DELTA TEACHER DEVELOPMENT SERIES

Series editors Mike Burghall and Lindsay Clandfield

The Business English Teacher

Professional principles and practical procedures

Debbie Barton • Jennifer Burkart • Caireen Sever

D1420078

Published by
DELTA PUBLISHING
Quince Cottage
Hoe Lane
Peaslake
Surrey GU5 9SW
England

www.deltapublishing.co.uk

© Delta Publishing 2010

First published 2010

ISBN 978-1-905085-34-7

Edited by Mike Burghall
Designed by Christine Cox
Cover photo © iStockphoto.com/Baloncici
Printed by Halstan & Co., Amersham, Bucks, England

Acknowledgements

We would like to thank all our past and present colleagues –
their ideas, creativity and enthusiasm have found their way
into this book in many ways.

Special thanks go to our colleagues at Linguarama Düsseldorf,
who inspired all three of us to make business English our
business, and to Mike, our editor, and Chris, our designer,
for their hard work and creative suggestions.

Finally, we would like to acknowledge each other – for great
team work throughout this project.

From the authors

All three of us are delighted to be professional business English teachers, and we wanted to share this enthusiasm with other teachers. Whether you are relatively new to teaching, whether you are coming from a general English background and now moving into business English teaching, or whether you already have some experience teaching business English but would like to do it in a more professional way, we hope to help you to successfully help your learners.

It is fulfilling for a teacher to work with business people on the skills they need to perform better in English. This book aims to make you less reliant on coursebooks and other published materials, and more confident using the learners' material as a basis for your courses. That material could be emails, documents or agendas supplied by them, details of phone calls they have made or need to make, presentations they write, or conversations about their business experiences. With such a wealth of relevant material, lessons are entertaining and, most of all, useful for the learner. As a teacher, there is nothing more rewarding than hearing about learners' real-life progress in English tasks – because they used to feel scared answering the phone in English but not longer do so, or they have recently taken part in a successful negotiation which they would not have been able to do before.

Teaching business English also offers you the opportunity to develop your own knowledge of business. Much of the conversation in the classroom requires you to ask questions about the learners' jobs and industries and, while they improve their English, you can learn from the experts who do these jobs every day.

You can also develop your teaching. Business English lessons can be as unpredictable as they can be exciting. Indeed, a privilege. Once freed from a syllabus imposed by a coursebook or other external source, you can experiment with various approaches which will most effectively help your learners to achieve their needs-based goals. Rather than teaching something just because it is 'in the book', you will be teaching what your learners actually need. How refreshing!

So, welcome to the world of professional business English teaching. You have a long journey to look forward to – with possibly a whole new career opening up – across many different industries, in the company of many different individuals and groups, with many different English needs.

Enjoy it!

Debbie Jennifer Caireen

Contents

Contents

Hi,

JCD International has just booked a course with us. Would you be interested in teaching it?

The learners are interested in presentation and negotiation skills, HR/finance vocabulary and speaking practice, with some focus on grammar. They are all of an intermediate level.

- The course will take place once a week for 20 weeks.
- The lessons are 90 minutes and scheduled for Thursdays at 4:00 pm at the company headquarters.
- At the end of the course, the company wants an assessment on the learners' progress and a levels update.

Please get back to me as soon as possible to let me know if you are able to take on the group.

Best regards,

The business English teacher

What, exactly, are business English teachers? We are just like any other teachers of English. We have qualifications; we have experience – we are *experts* at teaching the English language. Where our work is different is clear from the word 'business'. The business context brings new aspects into our teaching: our learners are experts in *another* field and have high expectations for what will be done in their lessons.

The email opposite illustrates a little of what can be involved in teaching business English. It also illustrates the dilemma often facing general English teachers and the reason for writing this book. Imagine, for our purpose, that you work in a language school and have just received it from your Director of Studies. You have to decide, and quickly, whether you want to take on the course – or not.

For teachers who are new to the field of business English, this email might seem daunting. This is to be expected. Our teaching certificate covers teaching techniques and language awareness, but many of us have never had experience in giving a work-related presentation or taking part in a business negotiation. Some business English teachers have a background in business, but many of us do not. Being asked to teach financial vocabulary or the vocabulary of Human Resources might seem overwhelming.

Even if you are an experienced business English teacher, you might question if you want to accept this course. Perhaps you have taught presentation skills, but never negotiation skills. Or maybe you have a strong grasp of HR vocabulary but no idea about finance. For many teachers, it might seem unusual that it is the company who is asking for an update on learners' progress at the end of the course – What would you include in such a report?

The business English experience

Yet there is no reason why you shouldn't be able to teach this course both successfully and professionally – and fully enjoy the experience. So why not accept?

What you need to start with is a grasp of the 'bigger picture' of business English, including what is involved in teaching business English *learners* as well as the structure and content of business English *courses*.

With a practical understanding of these overriding principles, you will be able to undertake classroom activities effectively within your specific business English context. Let us begin, then, to compose this picture – by looking at *who* you will teach; and subsequently, *where*, *what* and *how* you will teach them.

What is needed is a grasp of the 'bigger picture'.

The overriding principles involve responding to the needs of the learners.

Who will you teach?

The majority of learners are 'business professionals'. However, you might also teach pre-experience learners or those seeking a qualification in business English.

Business professionals Business professionals work for companies and learn English for their immediate or future needs. They work in a variety of departments, such as HR, finance or sales, and at different levels in the company – admin staff, department heads, senior managers, even the Chief Executive Officer. Language skills vary and you should expect to teach a range of levels.

You could be teaching a mixture of groups and one-to-one classes. In groups, all members could be from one department or from a variety of departments. One-to-one learners are usually senior managers who, due to work commitments, often have 'flexi' courses – lessons which take place at different times and on different days.

When teaching business professionals, it is important to remember that they often do not have a lot of time. They are busy with their jobs and frequently with their families, and fitting in language learning can be challenging.

Pre-experience learners These are typically business students or business trainees. They have little or no experience working for companies and currently no specific work-related needs. They are learning English in order to prepare for their *future* careers. Courses may be compulsory or voluntary, and you should expect to have to mark papers and exams.

The groups are often larger; you could find yourself teaching between 25–30 learners. The courses tend to be more general and to focus on a wider variety of topics. The learners may be following a general business English coursebook or preparing for an exam.

Qualification seekers Exam-preparation courses are often sought out by learners, especially pre-experience learners, as they see passing exams, such as the Cambridge Business English Certificate (BEC), as something extra that they can add to their CVs.

Exam courses have a recognisable goal and this helps some learners to maintain motivation. Much time is, of necessity, spent on exam technique and exam practice.

Down to business

- Reflect back on our email scenario and imagine *who* you will be teaching at *JCD International* – business professionals who work in the field of finance and HR. Their jobs and levels in the company differ: some may be accountants and others lawyers: some will work in administration while others manage their department. In the light of this group profile, it is crucial to start considering what you have to bear in mind as you embark on the course. And perhaps undertake some research about their possible job specifications.
- Remember that their lessons are once a week at 4:00 pm. This is late in the afternoon – the learners might be tired and perhaps still distracted by what has been going on in their jobs. And they may be anxious about meeting you and having to speak English in front of their colleagues.

As a business English professional, you are going to have to keep your learners' needs in mind, motivate them and make them feel comfortable speaking English.

Where will you teach?

Business English courses take place in a variety of settings, including companies, language schools or institutions of further education.

Companies Most business English teaching takes place in-company. The company premises could be in an office block or in part of a manufacturing plant. Within each company, the facilities vary. Sometimes teaching takes place in meeting rooms, sometimes in offices;

The majority of learners are business professionals.

The teacher's job is that of business English professional.

Business English courses are carried out in a variety of settings.

However, most teaching takes place in-company.

sometimes there is state-of-the-art equipment, sometimes none at all. You need to be prepared for all eventualities.

Language schools Some courses take place in language schools. These include courses for individual learners who travel to the school for an intensive course, or open-group courses in which a variety of business people come together in the evening to learn English. Business English lessons in language schools usually take place in traditional classrooms where you should expect whiteboard/flipchart and CD players.

Further education You may teach at an Institution of Higher Education, working for a Language Centre or directly for a School of Business. This often means that you will be teaching pre-experience learners. When teaching for universities, you often have to share rooms and pre-book facilities.

Down to business

- Imagine travelling to *JCD International* in the afternoon. You will probably have to take public transport to the company and then head back to the language school or travel to another company. Such a mixture of teaching and travelling to various locations throughout the area is typical. So be prepared to wear comfortable but professional clothing and to carry your lesson materials and equipment with you.
- Be ready to make the *most* of the resources that are available, and make the *best* of situations where they are not. You will need to be adaptable, being able to teach with all the latest technology – and occasionally in situations where there may not even be a flipchart.

As a business English professional, it is your job to be organised and to handle whatever facilities you encounter.

What will you teach?

Facilities vary and course types vary.

Business skills and business vocabulary usually form the main course content.

When teaching business English, you deliver a variety of course types: on-going and intensive, group and one-to-one. Some language schools offer business English courses which are open to the general public. This might mean teaching a group of professionals from a variety of companies – and learners who don't yet work for any company at all.

Whichever course you teach, the focus should always be on your learners' needs. Of these, the most likely areas to be taught will be business skills and business vocabulary. In our original email scenario, the learners of *JCD International* have requested the business skills of presentations and negotiations and the business vocabulary of HR and finance.

Other areas are very similar to any English teaching syllabus – the language *skills* of reading, writing, listening and speaking, plus language *systems* including grammatical structures and aspects of phonology.

Strategies that promote learner autonomy – to equip learners with the skills they need so that they can effectively continue to learn *outside* the classroom – are increasingly recognised as important features of a business English course, to the point that we can seriously consider them as part and parcel of the 'what' you will be teaching.

Business skills These involve the practical things that business professionals have to do in their working lives in English – giving presentations, participating in meetings and negotiations, telephoning, writing emails and socialising with business contacts. They form the main content of a business English course. But 'business skills' lessons, of course, include teaching the following elements of language:

- Functional language specific to the business skill, eg standard phrases for writing emails or taking part in meetings
- Language skills specific to that business skill, eg listening skills for telephoning in English or fluency for taking part in meetings

- Language systems specific to the business skill, eg pronunciation and intonation for giving presentations or modal verbs for being polite when telephoning.

Teaching business skills also involves looking at aspects of register and cultural awareness:

- 'Register' refers to how formal or casual a person's language is. For example, when teaching emails, a focus on the difference between formal and informal emails enables learners to write successfully for a variety of readers.
- Incorporating aspects of cross-cultural communication can help learners to become more aware of the problems that might occur when doing international business – and of strategies for avoiding them.

Business vocabulary This is the vocabulary and lexical chunks that learners need when doing their jobs in English. Typically, business vocabulary falls into the following categories:

- **General business vocabulary** What you would expect to find in a business English coursebook – vocabulary related to meetings (*minutes* and *agendas*) or vocabulary to describe trends (*increase* and *decrease*). These words are often familiar to all English speakers, even if they do not have a background in business.
- **Specialist vocabulary** Words very specific to your learners' jobs and the industry they work in (eg financial terms for a banker). This is vocabulary that you may not be familiar with yourself. Specialist vocabulary often cannot be found in coursebooks, so you have to rely on and exploit what you research and what your learners give you – emails, in-house magazines, annual reports, minutes and company websites and extranet/intranets.
- **Lexical chunks** Collocations, multi-word verbs and idioms that are crucial to business learners, especially when communicating with native speakers. When focusing on HR vocabulary, for example, you will look at collocations (*reject/hire an applicant*), multi-word verbs (*take on new staff*) and idioms (*a golden handshake*).

Language skills Learners ask for speaking, listening, reading and writing practice. Of these four skills, the most requested is speaking for a number of reasons:

- In the business world, learners need to be confident when communicating.
- Speaking is the most difficult skill to learn without practising with others.

When focusing on speaking skills you need to decide whether to do so in a business or in a general context – speaking about business topics (what is going on at the learners' company) or about general topics (what's in the news).

However, listening, reading and writing practice should also be integrated into your course so that your lessons have a balance of all four skills.

Grammar The amount of grammar taught also depends on the learners' needs. For example:

- A receptionist answering the phone and putting callers through probably needs to focus on functional phrases for telephoning rather than grammar.
- A business student who is applying for a job may benefit from reviewing tenses, as many multi-national companies check applicants' English through placement tests, which often include assessing knowledge of grammatical structures.

Focusing on grammar can make some learners feel more confident, especially those who are afraid of making mistakes. Grammar also meets some learners' expectations of what should be taught on their course – and they will request it. Whatever the learners' situations, their needs are best served by integrating grammar into the *skills* they need. For example:

- When asking for information via emails, you can focus on polite questions.
- A focus on the present perfect and past simple is a natural part of socialising.

Phonology Aspects of phonology help business English learners to pronounce individual words correctly, break up speech into appropriate phrases (phonological chunking) and use stress to highlight key words (sentence stress).

- When presenting, learners need to practise pausing to emphasise key points.

Language skills and language systems should also be integrated.

A balance should be achieved and, at the same time, expectations should be met.

- They benefit from focusing on intonation to effectively show interest when socialising, and to use the correct intonation pattern when asking questions.

If learners deal with native speakers, issues surrounding connected speech (linking words and elision, for example) are important to aid their understanding.

Down to business

- Refer back to the original email scenario and reflect on *what* you will teach at *JCD International*. The learners will want to do their jobs better. They will want to practise giving real presentations or taking part in negotiations similar to the ones that they are involved in. They will want to learn the HR and finance vocabulary that they can use when discussing their work. Furthermore, they will want to be able to express themselves clearly and accurately, and to feel confident when using English in work situations.
- Remember that business learners are often very goal-oriented people who expect to *learn* something work-related during lessons. They want to leave the room more *aware* of something and better able *to do* something related to their current or future jobs, otherwise they will feel that your lesson was not a good use of their time or company money.

As a business English professional, it is your job to meet these specific needs. How?

It is the business English professional's job to meet authentic needs.

These needs are both specific and work-related.

How will you teach?

Once you have considered who, where and what you are going to teach, you need to start thinking about *how* you are going to teach it. If you are new to business English, you may be wondering why you can't just give your learners a coursebook. Unless you are teaching pre-experience learners or qualification seekers, this is simply not the best option.

In our initial scenario, *JCD International* booked a block of twenty 90-minute lessons. It isn't realistically possible to finish a book within 20 lessons, nor will all the topics in a coursebook be relevant to your learners' needs.

To effectively teach business professionals, you need to go beyond the coursebook approach to teaching. This requires doing the following:

1 Deciding overall course objectives and individual lesson aims
2 Planning effective lessons
3 Giving feedback
4 Assessing progress
5 Checking satisfaction
6 Being prepared to deal with the unexpected

Through such careful consideration, you will not only deliver lessons that are professional but also lessons that more than meet your learners' expectations.

1 Course objectives and lesson aims

We have pointed out that the key to teaching business English successfully is to create your lessons around your learners' needs. Therefore, when deciding on the course objectives and the aims of each and every lesson, always put these as your first priority. Remember that your learners want to leave the room feeling that time has been well-spent, that they have learned and/or practised something related to their jobs.

Individual lesson aims must contribute to the overall course objectives.

Time must be seen to be well-spent.

To give learners this feeling, you need to have a good understanding of their work and why they are learning English. You should regularly go back and discuss with them their needs and where they feel they are making progress. There are several ways to do this. At the beginning of the course, you can conduct a needs analysis and, as the course progresses, you get the learners to complete self-evaluation sheets. You can also informally ask questions at the beginning of the lesson: 'Did you use English last week? What went well? What could have been better? How have the lessons helped you so far?' The information you obtain informs, literally, both the course and individual lesson.

Course objectives Objectives are long-term goals. For example, for the group in our original *JCD International* scenario, the course objectives can include:

- To be able to talk about jobs and responsibilities
- To extend the range of finance and HR vocabulary
- To be able to give a presentation about company products
- To be able to participate in negotiations about work-related topics

Objectives for a course should be agreed at the beginning and then reviewed regularly to take account of *changing* needs: the course objectives agreed with your learners dictate the aims of subsequent lessons. It is important to get consensus by discussing areas of disagreement when establishing course objectives. If the learners want to focus on different specialist vocabulary then it is necessary to agree that the course will look at general areas – as well as strategies which can be transferred to learning specific vocabulary.

Lesson aims Every lesson needs aims which are clearly defined and communicated to the learners. The aims should be seen to contribute to the achievement of the overall course objectives. When formulating aims, there are many points to consider – the level of the learners, their needs, any previous knowledge, etc.

Aims can be expressed in different ways. For example, as *objectives* or as *outcomes*:

- To introduce and practise vocabulary for financial statements
- By the end of the lesson the learners will have learned and practised vocabulary for financial statements

Whatever format is used, it is important not to have too many aims in one lesson and to make sure that they are specific, measurable and achievable.

2 Effective lessons

Time is precious for very busy business people. Therefore, you should not only have clear lesson aims but also a lesson plan that enables you to achieve them. To do this, you need to decide the following:

- What is the best approach to use, in order to achieve your lesson aims?
- What materials should you select to maximise classroom time?
- What is the best way to exploit the available resources and equipment?

Any approach can be used, as long as it is useful for the learners.

Tasks should be learner-centred and involve learners actively using the language.

Choosing your approach When doing your initial training, you were probably exposed to a variety of ways to focus on language. Any approach can be used with business English, as long as it is appropriate and useful *for the learners*.

Because the majority of learners need English to communicate, the communicative approach (Communicative Language Teaching) is most frequently used. CLT places great emphasis on interaction, on helping students use the target language in a variety of contexts and on learning language functions. Typical activities in a communicative business English lesson include pairwork, information-gap activities, roleplays and simulations. Such tasks can be approached in two ways:

- **Present-Practise-Produce** You can use conventional PPP-style lessons, first teaching language and then getting the learners to practise it. When focusing on telephoning skills you would first teach *functional phrases* for telephoning and then get the learners to *practise* the phrases through roleplays. Such lessons normally introduce language items by focusing on form, meaning and pronunciation, and contain both controlled and freer practice.
- **Test-Teach-Test** You will most likely find that learners respond better to TTT-style lessons, where you first 'test' their language abilities to find out what they already know. With telephoning skills, you would begin by having learners take part in the telephoning roleplay to *test* what specific language they already know. Then you *teach* the phrases they need to perform the task better and, finally, give them further practice by having them do the roleplay again (a second *test*). This

approach saves time because there is no need to teach language that learners already know and it gives them an opportunity to measure their progress.

Whatever you do, make sure activities are learner-centred. By this, we mean tasks in which the learners are actively *using* the language, as opposed to you teaching *about* language.

- Business skills tasks include business roleplays, discussions and presentations.
- Business vocabulary tasks include brainstorming words around a topic, finding collocations for specific words or predicting words that might appear in a text.
- Grammar activities might have learners give a short presentation on a topic in which they should use a particular structure, like talking about a finished project to test or practise past tenses.

And you should take the following into consideration – you will see that the strategies are reassuringly recognisable from most general English classes.

- Offer as much speaking practice as possible. Group discussions and pair discussions are invaluable. However, the learners should always have a recognisable aim and you should always give feedback: error-correction or suggestions of better language they could have used. This will make sure that a discussion is also a learning experience and not just a 'good chat'.
- Take on a monitoring role. This can be challenging when working with groups, as learners may feel more comfortable talking to *you* as opposed to talking to a partner or in a small group. Remind them that the goal of the lessons is to give them the opportunity to speak English and if they work in small groups, they will get to practise their English more. You may need to sit in the back of the room or even leave the room for a few minutes so that they get used to working in groups.
- Do review activities. These can include a quick vocabulary check at the beginning of the lesson or getting the learners to revisit a task that was done in a previous lesson. This will enable them to check that they have learned what has been covered and will give them the feeling that they are making progress.
- Plan for learners to do as much work as possible outside the classroom. If you are going to be teaching a grammar lesson, they could do some initial research using the internet or a grammar reference book. If you are going to talk about a current topic, they could read an article or watch a TV documentary at home and be prepared to talk about it in the lesson.

However, the challenge of creating interaction between learners of different hierarchies within a company should not be neglected. The business world is a competitive world.

Selecting your materials When planning their lessons, teachers who are just starting out in business English often turn to the first coursebook on the shelf, find a chapter that covers a topic which the learners have requested and then make copies. The main problems with doing this are that the chapter may not exactly address your learners' needs and as a result they may leave your lesson feeling as if they have wasted their time. In addition, some teachers plough through the whole chapter rather than selecting and exploiting the key activities.

When choosing materials, you may have the freedom to choose anything suitable. However, this freedom brings certain responsibilities with it. It can take time to search for materials and then to adapt and write activities to go with them. It can be difficult to know exactly what materials will help your learners. It is also common for less experienced teachers to over-prepare – and give their learners piles of handouts every lesson.

Some helpful guidelines are as follows:

- Put the responsibility on your learners by asking *them* to bring in materials for a future lesson. Examine the materials carefully, so that your planning is fully informed.
- Once you have a piece of material, exploit it as much as possible. Think about the grammatical structures it contains, its vocabulary and related issues such as

Reassuringly, business English and general English have many points in common.

The mix of hierarchies in a group, however, may present a challenge.

Lessons should be needs-driven, not materials-driven.

Freedom of choice involves greater responsibility.

pronunciation, register and different reading/writing skills that could be covered.

- Be needs-driven, not materials-driven. If you teach more than one learner at the same company and want to use material and activities with *all* of them, check first. Do they really need this lesson? Is it relevant? If it is, make any adaptations to ensure that the lesson matches each learner or group as closely as possible.
- Remember: less is more. Every lesson does not have to be based on handouts. 'Frameworks' (more on page 23) can lead to lengthy and worthwhile discussions. Learners also might want to hear from each other, especially if they are working in different departments in the same company and are genuinely interested in what others are working on at that moment. Real information gaps will lead to meaningful, learner-centred discussion.
- Don't forget: your business learners may attend several training seminars a year in which receiving PowerPoint handouts and handbooks is the norm. So make sure any handouts look professional. This includes good quality photocopies.

The range of business teaching environments implies vastly different resources being available.

Each resource used must help learning take place.

Exploiting your resources Another aspect to consider when planning lessons is the resources you have access to. Due to the range of business teaching environments, you often have hugely different resources available. You may find yourself in a conference room with the latest technology, including an electronic whiteboard. You may find yourself with only a flipchart. When teaching individuals, the lessons may take place in the learners' offices and all you have is a piece of paper to write on. Language schools and universities vary as well: some have up-to-date resources and others do not. When teaching in-company, you have to carry some of your resources with you, such as an MP3 player or video camera.

To make the most out of the resources that you have available, think about the following:

- How will each resource *help learning* take place? Integrating technology into lessons can make lessons more authentic and valid for your learners. However, this should be balanced with time constraints, as sometimes it is more efficient and effective to simply write something on a piece of paper or a flipchart.
- How familiar are you with the resources? If you are not comfortable with working with high-tech resources such as interactive whiteboards, we highly recommend getting some training on using them.

The result? More professional lessons and learners' expectations met!

3 Feedback

Feedback is essential for helping business English learners improve their language skills, as with any other learners. There are several strategies for giving feedback: immediate feedback, feedback sheets and performance criteria. Which strategy you use depends on the level of the learners, the aim of the lesson and when it is done within the lesson. But perhaps more importantly in our context: *who* you are teaching.

Feedback can be given in a variety of ways.

Sensitivity to the learners' culture is important.

Immediate feedback Immediate feedback is essential in the practice stage of a PPP lesson and the second part of a TTT lesson. It is also useful for error-correction. It definitely has a place with persistent or fossilised errors, and errors which cause real misunderstanding. For example: 'How long do you live here?' (Does this person mean *How long have you lived here?* or *How long are you going to live here?*) Such mistakes can often be due to first language interference or is one that the learner has been making for some time without being corrected. There are a number of techniques you can apply:

Echoing Repeating the mistake, to encourage the learner to say it again correctly.
Learner: *I have come to work yesterday.*
Teacher: *have come?*
Learner: *I came to work yesterday.*
Reformulating Repeating what the learner has said – but in a correct way.
Learner: *I have come to work yesterday.*
Teacher: *Oh, you **came** to work yesterday, did you?*

Gesturing Showing by a movement or facial expression that the utterance contains an error, and encouraging the learner to correct.

Signalling Having a special signal to indicate that the learner has made the same mistake again, or even holding up an object or a piece of coloured card every time the learner makes that mistake, and encouraging them to self-correct.

With business professionals, you may encounter some problems with immediate feedback. For example, in some cultures learners may be sensitive to being corrected. And where a group consists of line-managers and the people who report directly to them, the managers may not like being corrected in front of their staff – and vice-versa.

In such situations, it is important to address the issue openly. During discussions on correction, explain your rationale for correction and remind the learners that making errors is positive, as they enable you to ascertain the language areas where they need to improve. If they keep to simple language they are confident with, they will never improve, and making errors in the lesson enables you to give feedback and to correct them before they try out this language in the workplace.

Feedback should be on good points, and not just mistakes.

Mistakes are better made in class than in the work-place.

Feedback sheets These are simple forms used for noting both what the learners do well in a task and where they can improve. You can find examples of feedback sheets in many resource packs or teacher's books. Typically, they look like this:

Good language	Language that can be improved
I'll look into it and call you back.	I want to speak to Horst.

When using feedback sheets, the following is important:
- Avoid being too 'mistake-oriented' – only writing down grammar or pronunciation errors that you hear.
- Note good language used – including the language of the lesson as well as that covered previously.
- Record functional phrases and vocabulary that learners could use to do a task more effectively – especially important when doing TTT lessons.
- Notice learners' awareness of register and cultural issues – fundamental in business situations.

At the end of the lesson, or in feedback slots at the end of each fluency activity, go through your notes with the learners. If there is a photocopier close by, then make a copy for each learner. If not, write the areas that you want to highlight on the whiteboard or flipchart.

The advantages of using feedback sheets are that fluency is unaffected and learners receive a written record that they can use for reviewing. The disadvantage is that learners may stop speaking as soon as you start writing and want to know what the mistake was. You should remind them that you are writing down good language and new vocabulary as well as not-so-good language, and assure them that you will show them what you have written later.

Performance criteria You can give learners a task and then give feedback on their performance based on specific criteria. When focusing on presentation skills, come up with a list of criteria for giving feedback. This could include aspects such as:
- Having a clear structure
- Using signposting language
- Having good eye contact

The learners give their presentations and get constructive feedback on where they can improve based on the established criteria.

Performance criteria feedback is especially important when teaching qualification seekers, as they will need to know what criteria they are being assessed against when doing an exam. In the Cambridge BEC, for example, several areas for speaking are evaluated:

- Grammar and vocabulary (appropriacy and accuracy)
- Discourse management (range and appropriacy of structures and cohesion)
- Pronunciation (individual sounds and stress patterns)
- Interactive communication (turn-taking, positive contribution)

Criteria need to be clearly explained or negotiated with the learners, who need concrete feedback on where they can improve:
- Get them to produce a list that *they* think is important when evaluating their performance on a specific business skill and use their criteria to give feedback.
- Ask them to use the criteria to give peer feedback. Business English learners often find this approach motivating.
- Combine it with recording or videoing your learners. Record them giving a presentation and get them to listen and assess their performance. This is a good tool for raising awareness and for setting goals for future lessons.

The criteria for feedback and learner performance can be negotiated.

That said, as far as teaching is concerned, the teacher is the expert.

If you are just starting out teaching business English, it can feel uncomfortable to give feedback to someone who is a senior manager, both older and more experienced than you. If you have any doubts about how and when to give feedback, then ask your learners.
- In terms of error-correction, ask them at the start of the course how and how often they expect you to correct them, ask them again at the end of the lesson, and ask them again in their interim feedback and review sessions. Don't wait until it is too late to do anything about it.
- Before learners do a task, ask them what they would like to focus on and give feedback based on what *they* consider important.

Self-evaluation However, feedback is not exclusively in one direction only. Self-evaluation sheets can be completed by learners after they have done a task in English.
- It could be in a lesson – after a roleplay.
- It could be a task at work – after a presentation to clients, the learners ask themselves 'What went well?' or 'Did I effectively use signposting language?'

Self-evaluation is important because the learners are reflecting on their progress and taking an active part in their learning. By evaluating their performance themselves, they can give you feedback – important information to help when planning future lessons and establishing new objectives. Admitting difficulty answering questions after a presentation would lead to a lesson introducing and practising functional phrases to handle questions effectively.

In short, the more your feedback is a dialogue with your learners, the easier it will become to give them the information that they need to improve.

4 Learner progress

In our initial email, *JCD International* wanted an assessment on the learners' progress. This is normally in the form of a report in which you have to define where the individual learners made progress and if their overall level increased. The methods of checking include monitoring during lessons, self-assessment and informal tests. It is important to keep track of the information you accumulate so that you can write your report at the end of the course.

Assessment of progress is of importance to employers, not only to learners.

Progress should be carefully monitored and identified.

Monitoring Notes could be made during fluency activities or in more structured activities – something the learner does well or an area you notice they still need to develop. Use dates on your notes so that you can identify progress. Your notes might look something like this:

Gilbert

20 Oct: *Quite hesitant when speaking, taking a long time to give his opinion.*

9 Nov: *Used really good financial vocabulary from last lesson.*

23 Nov: *A well-prepared presentation on banking. Needs to work on sentence stress.*

30 Nov: *Used phrases well in discussion about company changes. Much more fluent.*

From these notes you can remind yourself at the end of the course what Gilbert can do well and where he has improved – and throughout the course to help you identify areas where he needs to develop.

Assessment is not exclusively in one direction only.

Self-evaluation sheets can be completed by the learners.

Self-assessment Learners often have a good idea of areas where they have progressed – when they are less nervous about telephoning with a British colleague or when they find it easier to understand people in meetings. Asking them how they see their own progress can also help you collect valuable information for the report-writing stage.

To do this, give the learners a self-assessment form. It is helpful to tailor these forms for each group or learner, with questions relating to areas you have covered on the course. Use 'can do' statements based on what you have covered, then the learners read the list and tick statements they feel apply to them:

- I can deal with phone calls asking for simple information.
- I can welcome visitors and show them to the waiting room.

An alternative is to use statements with a variety of answers for the learners to describe how well they can do each task:

	Very well	OK	Not very well	Not at all
Take a message from a courier				
Pass on a message about a late delivery				
Welcome visitors and show them to the CEO's office				

Informal assessment Informal tests are a good way to check what learners have learned. You can write the tests yourself and do them regularly, as well as at the end of the course. In the business world, the goal of such tests is not usually to give learners a mark, as it would be in the school system: it is to assess where they have made progress and to give feedback on where improvement is still needed.

An informal test can take several forms – such as multiple-choice, fill-the-gap or matching.

- The easiest things to test are grammar and lexis because they fit comfortably into the forms suggested above.
- However, you also need to test the business skills covered on your course, like telephoning. This can be done by getting the learners to revisit roleplays and reflecting on what they can do better now.

Progress is often better assessed in terms of specific areas than in traditional levels.

Assessment may have serious consequences in the work environment.

As with general English classes, when teaching business professionals you can get them to mark their own tests, instead of you telling them the answers. This will get them to think about where they have made progress – and where not. They can also work in pairs and compare their answers, trying to work out who is right when they have differences, which might make the correct answers more memorable and meaningful.

Formal assessment The information about the learners' level that you supply to the company might be used in an appraisal or go into their file for future reference – if a promotion comes up. You should include information about the level at the beginning of the course and the level at the end. Many language schools and many companies have their own level system and you will be expected to use it. Also – especially in some countries – you may be asked to use the Common European Framework (CEF) system.

Many factors will affect how much each learner's level increases:

- What was their initial level?
- How regularly did they attend lessons?
- How regularly did they complete self-study tasks?
- Did they try to find ways of increasing their exposure to English between lessons?
- How much do they use English in their everyday working life?

As business English courses typically only take place once a week, you may not see huge improvements in 'level'. Therefore it is often helpful to talk about progress in terms of *specific areas* – their ability to handle telephone calls – as opposed to their 'level' increase.

5 Learner satisfaction

Feedback on learners' satisfaction may be required by the language school, by the company, or both. You shouldn't be alarmed by this: if you have kept your learners' needs at the forefront of the lessons and maintained a dialogue with the participants, you should have nothing to worry about. Typical questions might be:

- How useful did you find these lessons?
- Do you now feel better able to use English in your job?
- Was there enough variety in the activities during the course?
- Would you recommend this course to a colleague?

It is especially useful to leave space for the learners to add comments:

- What was the most useful part of the course for you?
- What would have made the course better for you?

Even if it is not formally required, it might be a good idea to devise your own feedback form to collect information on what you did well and areas to think about on future courses.

Feedback forms are often completed in the final lesson of a course and collected immediately. However, some learners are more likely to give honest feedback if this is anonymous and posted or sent by email after the course has finished. The main disadvantage to this method, of course, is that you are not guaranteed to receive feedback from all the learners and you cannot ask questions to find out why the learners reacted as they did.

Whatever you do to assess progress, update levels or check satisfaction, make sure you prepare the learners, have clear criteria and make the criteria known.

6 The unexpected

However well-prepared you are, unexpected things happen to the business English teacher, and this means being flexible and reacting in a 'professional' way.

- You have prepared a careful 90-minute lesson on a grammar point (which was the next item on your programme), but when your one-to-one learner arrives they can only stay for 30 minutes because of an important meeting. Do you start your lesson and continue it next time or spend the 30 minutes doing something else – finding out more about that urgent meeting or talking about other current business activities?
- A learner comes to the lesson with a request to go through a presentation or prepare for a meeting, rather than do what you have prepared. Sometimes you might be able to take the information away and use it to prepare for a subsequent lesson, but the need may be more urgent. What would the learner like you to do? What do the other learners want? Listen to the presentation and give feedback? Check the presentation for accuracy? Roleplay the meeting? Help with vocabulary?
- You prepare a lesson for five learners but only one attends. What do you do?

Whenever unforeseen situations arise, the most important thing is still that you meet the needs of the learners. Ask them what they would like to do. In the last situation above, being able to make good use of resources available to you – using your learner's laptop to look at their company website or to talk about the emails in their in-box – will help you deal with this situation. Being informed about current business affairs and events in the company where you are teaching will allow you to have a work-related discussion, which business learners often appreciate.

Down to teaching business

So, now that you have the bigger picture of teaching business English, it should be no problem for you – when you read this new email from your DoS:

Hi,

Thanks for agreeing to take the class at JCD International.

In the first lesson, could you agree course objectives, check levels and get back to me with any problems? We want to send this to the company quickly.

This is a new, potentially key client and we want to make a good impression from the start.

I will be in touch with more information by the end of the week. In the meantime, please get back to me if you have any questions or concerns.

Best regards,

An understanding of the big picture will underpin a successful business English courses.

The next step is to concentrate on your detailed course preparation.

In Chapter 1 of Part B, we will be looking at how you can fill in the picture. It is time to get down to the business of detailed preparation and concentrate on the course:

- Use any information that you get from your DoS (if of course you have one) to start putting together your course objectives. Remember that you will need to include business skills and business vocabulary and to integrate language skills and language systems.
- Confirm with your DoS how you are expected to keep track of learners' progress and what type of report the company will want at the end of the course. Also find out if you will be expected to use a specific levels system.
- Think about how you will promote learner autonomy in the classroom and what strategies you will use to give feedback.
- Learn as much as you can about the company. Look at their website, find information on the internet, research the company's product or service and start consulting the meaning of specialist vocabulary.
- Look through all your materials and have ready everything you might.
- Check the details: times, number of learners, lesson length, even transport – How will you get there?
- Be prepared for problems. Make sure you know the name of the contact person in-company and always have a way of contacting your DoS.

We began talking about expertise. Business professionals do not expect you to be experts in their professional fields, but they do expect you to be effective in teaching the *language* of their fields. We hope the activities in Part B of *The Business English Teacher* will help to put together effective and expert lessons for your learners.

So do your homework. Be prepared. And make the most of the challenging variations and variables afforded by each business English teaching situation. Now would seem to be a good moment to focus on these variations and variables:

Courses – What you teach and who you teach

Sources and resources – What you teach with and how you teach with it

Courses

Courses and classes will vary and learners will be varied. The principles and practice presented in Part B of *The Business English Teacher* amply address the needs of intermediate learners – it would seem worthwhile, therefore, to answer a number of frequently asked questions of particular interest in other business English contexts.

Beginners

Don't all beginners have the same needs? All beginners need to learn largely the same basic vocabulary, grammar and pronunciation, and it may be a good idea to use a coursebook to give support. However, you should still adapt materials and supplement the basic structures and vocabulary with any work-related tasks your learners need to accomplish. Even beginners may be expected to carry out tasks in English. Someone who has to answer the phone will need a few basic phrases and listening practice for potential calls.

- Do this classroom practice *before* they tackle any of the grammar and vocabulary areas which usually form parts of a beginner syllabus.
- Remember that even if you are following a coursebook, you can still incorporate extra examples of work-related vocabulary.

What should I teach them? It is still important to do a needs analysis and to write your course aims, although you may have to do this in their first language (if you can). If following a coursebook, keep referring to these aims to make sure that what *you* are teaching is what *they* need to learn – concentrate on vocabulary and functional phrases rather than grammar:

- Give them useful expressions to say (or write, if that is the task they have to perform).
- Check they can pronounce them and know when to use them.
- Do drills and simple roleplays to build up confidence.

Teaching learner autonomy is also vital at this level:

- Show them how to use a dictionary properly.
- Suggest they make their own reference lists of phrases.

Should I use their first language? There is no right or wrong answer to this and it is natural for people, especially at lower levels, to translate into their own language.

- For some learners, it is reassuring to know that their teacher can understand them if they have a real difficulty. Definitions for new vocabulary should always be given in English, but you can ask for *their* language word as well, to double-check.

- Even a simple task such as explaining why they can't be in the lesson next week gives learners the chance to practise English for real communication. Using their first language will deprive them of the opportunity to listen to or use English.

Advanced

What is there left to teach advanced learners? Learners at advanced levels can usually do 'what' they want in English, but they may need help extending 'how' they do it – increasing their range of formal language, improving intonation when giving a presentation. What exactly do they want to improve?

- Do they have a concrete goal – a negotiation?
- Do they want to improve a specific area – report writing perhaps?

Pay careful attention to *what* they say and *how* they say it – record them, if possible, to look later for fossilised errors or other problem areas they are unaware of.

What strategies work? The learners have already come a long way in their language learning so they clearly know some learning strategies which work for them. Talk about this and build on their current good practice – suggest podcasts they could download, show them a monolingual dictionary they haven't seen before. You could say your role is more facilitator than teacher.

You will almost definitely not be using a coursebook, as they rarely fit the specific needs of advanced learners.

- Obtain authentic material – confront them with more complex news articles and longer broadcasts.
- Take them out of their language 'comfort zone' – with challenging discussions and case studies.

There will rarely be a specific focus on grammar with advanced learners – 'accuracy' will be integrated into the error-correction sections of your lessons, but if they do want to look into a grammar area you can of course cover this.

Mixed groups

What are mixed groups? In an ideal world, all your groups would consist of people with the same jobs, the same learning needs and expectations and the same level of English. However, in many companies, groups contain less than ideal dichotomies of 'levels':

- Seniority – secretaries and administrative staff, middle managers and senior managers, directors and vice-presidents
- Language – the levels of English commonly termed 'beginner to advanced'

Courses

How can I cater for everyone? Ensuring that the needs of all the learners in the group are addressed requires careful handling:

- Senior group members' needs must not dominate when discussing course objectives or doing activities. There could also be cultural issues here – so do research into your local context.
- Mixed language levels require you to give higher-level learners enough challenge, but not leave the lower levels feeling confused and frustrated. Think about your lesson objectives in a realistic way:
  - All learners must …
  - Some learners may …
  - A few learners might …

Set initial individualised goals and targets, then use self-assessment for each individual learner to decide to what extent they are achieving their targets.

- Exploit differentiated resources – allow lower-level learners to use bilingual dictionaries, or use two different versions of the same reading text.
- Set a different number of tasks – to be completed in the same amount of time.
- Set research tasks and homework tasks – allow learners to devote the time they need.
- Allow pair-checking before feedback – monitor who has the correct answer and ask less confident learners who you know have the right answer a difficult question. A great confidence booster!

Large groups

How big are big groups? A 'group' can be anything from two people, but in-company business lessons usually have a maximum of around eight – training officers realise that larger groups are less effective. However, there can be exceptions, especially pre-experience learners and 'open' groups in a language school.

What strategies can I use? Designing a course can be difficult when you have a lot of people with very different needs and expectations.

One strategy is to follow a coursebook – especially when your learners do very different jobs or work in different companies and have fairly general needs. A good business English coursebook covers a range of business skills and topics, as well as useful vocabulary and grammar points.

Do a needs analysis, but accept some negotiation when you decide on the course objectives – one person may request report writing while others may want speaking practice:

- Speak to the individual concerned and suggest some self-study ideas.

- Ask the whole group if they would be interested in report writing for part of the course, as it may be useful to them in the future.

Are there any benefits? You will always get a reasonable number of people attending the lesson!

- With small groups, you might plan a roleplay needing a minimum of four people and only two attend.
- With large groups, you have lots of options for interesting debates, roleplays, case studies and discussions, as well as competitive team games – there is a wealth of experience and opinion to bring into play.

One-to-one

Who does one-to-one lessons? Usually senior managers – people with specific needs who need to make very fast progress:

- These lessons are usually more expensive.
- The learners are very busy people with very high expectations.

How are they different? You can work on exactly what your learner needs as there are no other participants to take into consideration:

- Work with the learner's own work documents for example, emails and presentations.
- Focus on their individual problems – pronunciation, or lack of confidence when speaking up in a meeting.

You may need to prepare less beforehand, as the learner will talk about recent working experiences or bring in documents – but this means that you have to be very flexible and 'think on your feet'.

How can I provide variety? One-to-one lessons can be quite intense – there is no pairwork and you cannot change partners. To compensate:

- Use a variety of different activities – frameworks, card-matching, online resources.
- Include both audio and video listening – so the learner does not listen to only you.
- Move around – get them to stand up and write on the board or give you a presentation.
- Leave the room – let them prepare a presentation or read an article alone.

Can we do roleplays? In activities designed for pairs, you will have to take one of the roles, which can make it difficult to take notes for later feedback and error-correction.

- Record the roleplay.
- Use the recording as a basis for feedback.

Courses

Intensive

What is an intensive course? Learners with urgent needs or with working schedules that prevent having regular lessons might choose an intensive course. This often means lessons all day every day, for a week or sometimes longer. It will usually be one-to-one, but might involve small groups.

What will I do all that time? As always, a thorough needs analysis is vital. In the first session, you will probably talk about the learners' jobs and English needs – to decide what to do for the rest of the course.

- Divide the sessions up into different sections – one half of the morning practise telephoning language, the other half look at their emails.
- Include breaks – go for a coffee together, which will leave you refreshed when you come back to the class.
- Give the learners a self-study task – planning a presentation or watching a DVD – and leave the room.

What strategies work? Learners cover a lot of ground in a short time, so revision is essential for them to assimilate it. Encourage them to record new vocabulary and go through it together at the end of each day and at the start of the next.

- All the points made about creating variety in one-to-one lessons apply here, but you also have the luxury of time to get involved in more detailed tasks – writing a report or preparing a presentation.
- Record the learners on the first morning then use the recording to check progress at the end of the week.
- Talk extensively about how the learners can continue practising and improving their English – they may not be able to follow up the course with further lessons.

Long-term

How do the learners keep motivated? Group courses can run for a long period of time – even years – possibly with some learners joining and some leaving.

- Revisit the course objectives regularly and check if the learners want to amend or add to them.
- Refer to your course objectives when planning lessons, making sure they contribute to overall needs.
- Ask regularly for feedback on how the lessons are going and if any changes are needed.
- Check progress frequently and do self-evaluation tasks so they perceive their own progress.

How do I keep motivated? You may feel you have used up all your best ideas or are getting stuck in a rut when you have been teaching the same group for a long time.

- Checking progress regularly will help – nothing is more motivating than seeing learners make progress!
- Recordings from some time before which identify areas where learners have really improved remind everyone of what has been achieved.

One advantage is that you all know each other very well and you can exploit this in lessons. You probably understand perfectly what they do for their jobs and know a lot about the company, so can think of activities which directly relate to their work. Groups you know well can also be good for trying out something new – a new teaching approach, a new activity type or some new technology. This will keep your lessons fresh and help you to expand your repertoire.

Exam preparation

Who does business English exams? There are many and varied reasons for taking an examination in English:

- Pre-experience learners or trainees – to enhance their job prospects
- Employees – if being considered for promotion
- Other learners – simply to motivate themselves

What are the advantages and disadvantages? Exam courses have a recognisable goal and this helps teacher and learner maintain motivation.

The best business English exams test learners on very practical tasks which are useful in their working lives – writing emails or taking part in discussions. This means that exam training can have a positive effect, but it is not always perceived as such:

- Time is spent on exam technique and practice – some learners feel it could be better spent on more content.
- The exam might include topics and skills they do not need – perhaps writing reports or giving presentations – yet they have to master them for the exam.
- Exam teaching can feel more 'fixed' than non-exam teaching, especially as it usually uses a coursebook and has a prescribed syllabus – the course may seem inflexible, which could affect motivation.
- Exams cost money – some companies cover the costs, but in many cases learners have to pay for the exams themselves.

Which exams can I recommend? There are a lot of Business English exams. Probably the best known are Cambridge BEC and TOEIC, but there are others.

It is not for us to recommend an examination – you can find plenty of information on the internet, including tips for candidates, exam centres and costs.

Sources and resources

Materials from a multiple selection of sources will enable you to customise your course. And given the huge variations in 'classroom' situations in-company, it is important to investigate and exploit all the possible resources afforded by the individual environments.

Sources

■ **Authentic materials** These are up-to-date materials from newspapers, magazines, television and radio, and the internet. If you research the learners' company or industry, their website often contains press releases, descriptions of company activity and links to relevant news articles in English. Learners are motivated by talking about topics directly related to their jobs and such materials are a good source of specialist vocabulary. They can take a lot of time to convert into a practical lesson, but it is particularly well worth it if you are teaching several groups at the same company.

■ **Coursebooks** Working strictly from coursebooks is not suitable for most business professionals (the possible exception would be qualification seekers) but they can be a source of inspiration. You can adapt tasks so they are more suitable to the company where you are teaching, rewriting a meetings roleplay, for example, so that it is relevant to your learners' own meetings. It is important to ensure that your versions *look* professional and cite at the bottom of the page the source of the original task (so you are not breaking copyright laws).

■ **Dictionaries** Monolingual learner dictionaries (online, CD format and hard copy) promote learner autonomy. In lessons, learners can ask *you* the definition of a word or its pronunciation. In the office, they have to figure it out for themselves. Learner dictionaries enable them to do this efficiently without help and are a source of authentic examples of usage, which improves their ability to write, especially when dealing with verb patterns, prepositions and paraphrasing. However, you should be aware, too, of the existence and the potential in your lessons for the following:

- bilingual dictionaries
- collocations dictionaries
- idioms dictionaries
- specialist dictionaries

■ **Frameworks** These are worksheets with very little information, often in the form of tables, bullet-pointed boxes or flowcharts. They are a 'skeleton' source which the learners themselves can complete individually, making them personally relevant, or in pairs, practising a lot of work-specific language as they discuss what to include in the framework. You can easily adapt them so the focus is on what your learners need if you do the appropriate research beforehand.

■ **Photocopiables** Resource packs of material to be photocopied can include business skills, cultural awareness, discussion ideas, roleplays, pronunciation and vocabulary. The internet and some teacher's books also include photocopiable materials. They save preparation time and you might feel more confident with a commercially produced worksheet – they look very professional and could meet learners' expectations as to what business materials should look like in a business English lesson. The problem? They are standardised, often written for a global market. A resource pack roleplay can never be totally 'authentic', so you may finally have to rewrite or adapt it to make it more appropriate.

■ **Work documents** These are materials your learners give you. If they read reports in English, it is more 'authentic' to use those, rather than something *you* have found. If they write emails, which they no doubt do, you can start with some that *they* have written, identifying areas to work on and discovering what kind of emails they actually write. Other useful work materials include annual reports, minutes from meetings and presentation slides.

Resources

■ **BlackBerries/smartphones** Phones have always been perfect for telephone language – learners go to different offices and call each other. But a new generation of business English teachers and a new generation of learners can do infinitely more with this new generation of technology. They can take notes and record themselves, do agenda-type activities and show photos, download dictionary and other language learning 'apps' (software applications) to consult. Smartphones have web access – so queries and doubts can be checked on the internet during lessons, using sites in English.

■ **Cards** Learners can record new and useful language onto index cards to review at home or when on the move – they are more flexible than lists on paper or in a notebook. Teachers can focus on language, via roleplays or games which use cards in a variety of procedures. They can take time to prepare, so it is sensible to laminate them for durability.

■ **DVDs** Extracts from DVDs can be integrated into lessons. Parts of commercial films – a speech or a meeting – can highlight useful language or start a discussion. Financial reports, or films giving information on certain industries, are good for extended listening. For self-study, learners can watch films or television programmes in English, with or without subtitles.

Sources and resources

■ **Flipcharts** They can be a permanent record of what is written up in class. Pieces of flipchart paper displayed around the room allow learners to refer to them – for example after brainstorming a list of phrases for a discussion activity. Learners can also work in small groups and collect ideas on flipchart paper before presenting them to the whole group.

■ **Interactive whiteboards** IWBs have all the benefits of using a laptop and projector, with the added advantage of an interactive screen which you can write on and then save onto the computer. They are extremely versatile and easy to use by anyone who is familiar with using a computer.

■ **Internet** This is an obvious and increasingly important resource to exploit in the lesson – you can watch short videos and listen to radio or audio files, integrating these as listening activities or to begin a discussion. Also, there are websites specifically for learning English where you can direct your learners for self-study.

■ **Laptops** Whether your own or the learners', laptops are extremely useful for showing video clips and podcasts in lessons, for accessing work-related resources – for example, learners' own emails and PowerPoint presentations – or for presenting feedback and for learners to work on writing – emailing or writing up summaries and minutes after a roleplay. The learners can record new vocabulary directly onto their computer. Laptops are a particularly appropriate resource in one-to-one lessons.

■ **Listening devices** Cassette players look old-fashioned, which may not match the learners' expectations in companies with the latest IT equipment, but **cassettes** are still used by teachers to make recordings of learners giving presentations before giving feedback. **CDs** offer much better quality, and are a good source of self-study materials – learners can listen to business English CDs in their cars. However, they are only really useful when using published materials – being difficult for recording, requiring special equipment and some IT skills. There are not so many small portable CD players on the market, which is a problem if you have to travel. However, it is likely that a CD player will be available in-company.

■ **MP3 players** These are a fantastic resource – MP3 players and small portable speakers are becoming more accessible all the time. With access to a computer, you can store a large amount of listening material and carry it around easily. The quality is excellent. More and more authentic and TEFL material is available to download in the form of podcasts, and CDs can easily be converted into MP3 files. Small MP3 voice recorders are perfect for recording learners – the recordings can then be sent to them in an email or on a CD.

■ **Overhead projectors** (OHPs) and accompanying transparencies (OHTs) look a little old-fashioned now but in some environments nothing else is available. OHPs are especially useful for taking notes while monitoring during a fluency activity – before you show your notes to the group for correction together. OHTs can be pre-prepared as part of your lesson plans, with relevant visuals, and be given to learners as alternatives to flipcharts to summarise group discussions.

■ **Paper** Integrating technology into lessons can make lessons more authentic for your learners – but sometimes it is more efficient to simply explain something or write it on a piece of paper. Less is sometimes more! Every lesson need not be based on imported materials. How does what you use *help learning* take place?

■ **People** Your learners are your principle resource. They probably want to hear from each other – and are genuinely interested in what others are doing. You can simply facilitate the interaction and make some notes.

■ **Pinboards** These are good for brainstorming ideas, such as performance criteria or presentation content. The learners can work individually and write ideas for a topic on coloured cards then pin them up. The cards can be moved around and put into groups or categories, so that previously-hidden patterns emerge.

■ **Video cameras** You can film your learners giving a presentation or taking part in a meeting, and a short section can be used for feedback or self-evaluation. When watching, the learners notice their body language, as well as pronunciation and other areas which could be improved.

■ **Video projectors** You can give PowerPoint presentations yourself or give your learners practice. You can show internet pages to the whole group or show DVDs through your laptop or a portable DVD player.

■ **Whiteboards** They are not only for *you* to use! Your learners can stand at the whiteboard and make mindmaps or brainstorm ideas or answers together.

■ **Workplace** Finally, don't forget to exploit as a resource the place where your learners actually work. If they take visitors on company tours, they can take *you* on a tour. If they describe technical processes, they can take you into the factory and explain the processes. This is very motivating and gives you the opportunity to determine areas to work on in future lessons.

The Business English Teacher has looked at the challenging contrasts and reassuring similarities between business English and general English teaching. It is now the moment to put the strategies to the test. We think two points are worth making here:

- Confidence is all. In each of our three chapters, we begin by answering a series of 'frequently asked questions' that we hope will allay some of your apprehensions.
- Customisation is everything. Following the principle 'learner needs' – and also due to the contingencies of limited space! – the examples we propose throughout Part B are exactly that: examples. When preparing a questionnaire, a text, a roleplay or a card-sorting activity, you might like to take advantage of the examples we propose, but we are sure you will also want to want to formulate your own.

Business from the beginning

You need to have an overview of your objectives and obligations – before you can know what your individual lesson aims are going to be and can set about applying them. From the beginning, analyse your learners' needs, teach learner skills, maintain motivation and progress by adapting your lessons, reviewing and recycling the content – and finally finish off with a demonstration of what has been successfully achieved and what can still be done.

The language of business

Although, as a teacher of business English, you are not necessarily an expert in business – nor do you have to be – you are an expert in English. This means you don't tell business people how to do their jobs; rather, you let them tell you. What you provide is the language to enable them to use their business skills and expertise successfully – *the language of business*.

The business of language

While you will be providing your learners with the business language needed for their specific jobs, there will be times when you feel they need more. Competent users of English must function in a variety of situations and they may need to work specifically on language skills and language systems. Using authentic materials and teaching strategies like those suggested here, this is where you are definitely the expert – *the business of language*.

1 Business from the beginning	**2** The language of business	**3** The business of language
Learner needs	Telephoning	Frameworks
Learner autonomy	Emails	Authentic/work materials
Learner dictionaries	Presentations	Vocabulary
Learner progress	Meetings and discussions	Phonology
Learner success	Negotiating	Grammar
	Socialising	

Chapter 1
Business from the beginning

Introduction
- Learner needs
- Learner autonomy
- Learner dictionaries
- Learner progress
- Learner success

Introduction

We spoke earlier of the 'bigger picture' – how you need to concentrate on the course. It is now time to focus on the first lesson – to prepare for that first crucial encounter with your business learners. This includes:

- Prepare a lesson that will help you to get to know their jobs and needs, and activities to confirm and establish levels.
- Prepare a needs analysis to be able to set course objectives, and probing questions to get further information.
- Prepare to ask your learners for authentic material – work documents and websites.
- Prepare to check all available resources so that you can take advantage of them.

In this first lesson, you should be prepared to confront and negotiate important issues:

- Error-correction – how you will correct them
- Contact with English – outside your classroom
- Homework – benefits, time frames and tasks

Take homework, for example. In our experience, attitude varies. Some learners will do a lot, others will find it difficult to fit homework into their already busy schedules. Many might associate doing homework with how they learned English in school and may be reluctant. Remind them that doing it will help them to achieve their goals.

Do your needs analysis and ask how much time the learners think that they can *realistically* spend between lessons completing homework tasks. Encourage them to think about how they can increase their contact with English – read a book, listen to a CD in the car or watch the news. This will lead you gently on to the issue of learner autonomy.

Negotiate, discuss, approach the course in a businesslike way from the very beginning. Follow our overriding principle, which will determine how you proceed – your learners' needs. But remember: they might not always know what their needs are. Never forget: *you* are the expert as far as teaching is concerned. In Chapter 1, our first activity will be a needs analysis interview – before we move on to learner autonomy.

So, apply the principle, do your preparation – and proceed.

Learner needs

How do I know what business learners need? A thorough needs analysis interview at the beginning of a course supplies absolutely invaluable information for deciding on course objectives and lesson aims:

- Current and future use of English
- Skills and topics that learners would like to focus on
- Language learning preferences
- Strengths and weaknesses in the target language

Different institutions have different 'needs analysts':

- An administrator or senior teacher before the course begins – read their information carefully and *check* it with your learners during the first lesson to let them know that their needs will be the centre of the course.
- The teacher in the first lesson – get as much information before the course begins and do a needs analysis at the beginning of the course. Use questionnaires, checklists and interviews – giving the learners a chance to share their needs and agree common ground.

For some learners, it can be difficult to put their exact needs into words. They say they need to 'better' their English, but they aren't sure how. Ask 'probing questions' to find out all the information you need – What do they mean? Where do they speak? Who are they with? What isn't good enough? When was the last time they spoke English and felt this?

- A software developer who writes instruction manuals, reports and emails may rarely speak. A receptionist might greet visitors and answer the phone, but rarely write anything longer than a telephone message.
- The learners may need to make small talk with business partners, state an opinion convincingly in a meeting or answer unexpected questions at the end of a presentation.
- The problem may be vocabulary – they find it hard to speak because they don't know the right words. This could be work-related or general 'socialising' vocabulary.

Don't be afraid of spending plenty of time asking questions *throughout* the course (as these needs may well change) – the better you know their needs and their aims, the better you can achieve them.

Business from the beginning

Learner autonomy

How important is it? In business English, learners typically come for a fixed block of lessons which take place once a week. Attendance may be irregular due to the pressures of work, and they may go for long periods without lessons. You must equip them with strategies – learner autonomy means being independent learners – both during the course and when it is over:

- Effectively recording and reviewing new language
- Maintaining contact with English beyond the classroom
- Knowing how to use – and using – learner dictionaries

When do I start? So that learners get as much as possible out of the whole course:

- Focus on their autonomy from the very beginning – recording new language so they can systemically review it on their own.
- Introduce strategies for increasing contact with English – so they can try them out during the course and choose which ones they want to continue with.

What can they do? In non-English-speaking countries, there are many possibilities to have contact with English:

- **Reading and listening** News on satellite or cable television; DVDs in the original language, with or without subtitles; cinemas showing films with subtitles; radio, such as the BBC World Service; the internet (podcasts, etc); audio books; English learning websites (with grammar and vocabulary exercises); newspapers and magazines, in print or online; learner magazines or newspapers (with easier texts and help with vocabulary); graded readers.
- **Speaking** There are sometimes 'English speaking circles' set up so native speakers who have moved to the area can make friends, or so people learning English can meet up and practise.
- **Writing** Learners can email each other, especially if a course is finishing and they want to keep in touch. They can join chatrooms or discussion forums on the internet.

What can I do? Practise top-down listening and reading techniques to teach strategies which help learners feel confident to read and listen on their own. In addition:

- **Vocabulary** Show learners how to select vocabulary which is useful for them and then ways of learning it.
- **Business skills** Show them how to identify typical phrases related to their jobs – in emails they receive – and ways of learning them – keeping a list of useful telephoning phrases next to the phone.

Learner dictionaries

What are the advantages? Monolingual dictionaries are a great tool for promoting learner autonomy. In the classroom, learners can ask you for the definition or pronunciation of a word. In the office, they have to be able to figure them out on their own. Learner dictionaries enable them to do this without your help.

In addition, they allow the learners to see authentic examples of how words are used, to improve their ability to write and to get practice in paraphrasing the meanings.

How can I encourage my learners to use them?
Incorporate dictionary skills into your lessons regularly – to introduce new vocabulary and when giving error feedback:

- If you hear a mistake with the use of a preposition, encourage looking in the dictionaries for the correct choice.
- Get the learners to look in the dictionary when they don't know the meaning of a word, rather than just asking you.
- Encourage them to use dictionaries when they finish an in-class writing activity – to check spelling or verb patterns.

Finally, remember to transfer what you do in the classroom to what learners can do in the office – when focusing on stress patterns, remind them to use their dictionaries to check a word when preparing a presentation.

What about bilingual dictionaries? You may discover when checking learners' writing that they make a lot of lexical errors that come from using bilingual dictionaries. Most bilingual dictionaries only give translations of single words: they don't give collocations or other information about the word – how formal it is, for example. Learners easily choose the wrong translation, use the word with unusual-sounding collocations or use inappropriately formal language or slang. Point out such mistakes and explain how monolingual dictionaries can prevent them. Why not get the learners to look up a word in a bilingual dictionary, then use the monolingual dictionary to check that the English word is correct and see how it is used in a sentence?

What about online dictionaries? A good strategy is to use online monolingual learner dictionaries. There are several good ones on the internet and if learners use a bilingual dictionary to look up a word, they can then use one of these websites to check they are using and pronouncing it correctly. If you have access to internet in the classroom, why not encourage them to use these sites during activities?

Do I have to carry dictionaries with me? If you are doing a lot of in-company teaching, encourage learners to buy their own dictionary at the beginning of the course – and bring it to the lessons. Aternatively, if the rooms that you teach in have internet access, why not ask them to bring their laptops and then use online dictionaries? There are also electronic monolingual dictionaries that learners can install onto their laptops. If one-to-one lessons take place in the learner's office, use their computer.

Learner progress

How important is reviewing and recycling? As important as in any general English classes – perhaps more so. You will, however, find that most of what you do with your learners is already quite familiar:

Reviewing means going over language from previous lessons:
- Review vocabulary or grammar.
- Revisit your end-of-lesson feedback and corrections.
- Summarise a text you read last lesson or a report you listened to.
- Do a controlled-practice activity again in the next lesson, but with a shorter time limit.
- Remind the learners of strategies you discussed for increasing exposure to English between lessons.
- Review course content/learning objectives as part of planning for future lessons.

Recycling means re-using language from previous lessons:
- Follow a lesson on telephoning phrases with a different roleplay – so the learners can practise the phrases again.
- Follow a lesson on agreeing and disagreeing phrases with a discussion prompted by a text on a controversial issue.
- Set discussion questions using recently-acquired items of vocabulary.
- After a lesson – on signposting phrases for presenting – get the learners to prepare mini-presentations on a grammar point or on what they have learned.

When should I do it? You should do some reviewing in every lesson. Furthermore, it is good practice to have a 'review lesson' after approximately 16–20 hours of teaching. This gives you the opportunity to see what has been learned and if progress has been made. It allows you to review the original objectives – to discuss which ones have been met and which not, thus informing future planning.

How do I organise a review lesson? Tell the learners in advance to go back through their notes to prepare and perhaps ask them to bring their notes to the lesson.
- Start by talking about the course objectives and list what has been done towards achieving them.

- Do a variety of activities to review and recycle the materials.
- Get the learners to reflect on the course objectives again and to consider which ones they have achieved and which ones they still need to work on.

Review lessons can be fun. Use games – learners enjoy the competitive element and it makes it seem less like a 'test' situation.

How can I maximise their learning? To really make progress, learners need to be trained to do their *own* reviewing on a regular basis:
- Looking through their course notes before every lesson – and using self-study resources such as websites to work on any problematic areas.
- Implementing strategies for learning vocabulary – by using a box of index cards to record new words along with their definition in English or in translation, or storing them in virtual index files.

Part of *your* job is to give them these strategies for reviewing, and to motivate them to do it.

Learner success

What should I do before the last lesson? This depends on the requirements of the client and the school you are working for. In our initial email scenario, *JCD International* wanted an assessment of learners' progress and a levels update. Therefore there should be some form of exit test and an opportunity for learners to assess their own learning – *their* success – and to give feedback on the course – *your* success. These activities should take place *before* the last lesson so that the final lesson can be a celebration of the learners' hard work and achievements.

What should I do in the last lesson? Remind the learners of the objectives they set at the beginning of the course and what was done to achieve them. Revisit activities to show what progress has been made and discuss how they will continue their learning.

Needs analysis interview

Principle Learners, and one-to-one learners in particular, need a course specifically designed to help them meet their language learning requirements. Use 'open questions' to help you find out what they do and what their priorities and preferences are. With this information, you will better able to shape your future planning.

Prepare

If you find out as much as you can about the learner *before* the first lesson, this background information sets a context for you so their answers in the interview make more sense. If the organisation you work for did a needs analysis, make sure you read it carefully.

Have ready *English tick list* (see opposite) or *Priority cards* (page 31) as a back-up in case the learners have difficulty expressing their needs. For specific information about skills and language, see the 'probing questions' (page 30) to establish objectives.

Proceed

- Tell the learners that you need to find out as much as you can about their English needs to design the best course to help them.

- Ask a series of open questions (see page 30) and encourage the learners to speak as much as possible. Make notes during the discussion.

- Summarise what was discussed. Write down the main needs, to be able to refer to them throughout the course.

- Discuss how much time the learners have to do homework, and what activities they would find most useful.

- Ask them if they have any authentic materials of their own they can bring to the next lesson.

Alternative Give the learners a questionnaire *before* the first lesson so that they can start thinking about their needs and prepare for the discussion.

Review Refer back to the needs analysis at the start of your lessons as the course advances – *As we discussed in the first lesson, one of your needs is taking messages on the telephone, so today we are going to look at telephone language.*

English tick list

Principle Learners, especially business professionals, need to know the course will be designed around their work requirements. Individual interviews are difficult within groups, and some learners find it hard to answer open questions such as *What would you like to focus on?* Give extra support when discussing needs and priorities. 'Probing questions' (page 30) can then be asked, so you get all the information you need.

Prepare

Prepare your own tick list and make a copy for each learner.

Which areas of English do you to practise the most? Tick your 3–4 main priorities for the course.		
☐ Speaking	☐ Presentations	☐ Business vocabulary
☐ Writing	☐ Telephoning	☐ Technical vocabulary
☐ Listening	☐ Socialising	☐ Grammar
☐	☐	☐

In addition, prepare follow-up questions:
- If 'speaking' is a priority: Do they want to practise speaking about business topics or current events?
- If they want to focus on presentations: What was the last one they gave? What do they find difficult about giving presentations in English?

Proceed

- Explain the rationale for your tick list.

- Give out the list and ask the learners to decide individually their main three or four priorities. Set a time limit.

- When the learners report back, ask probing questions to find out more about their needs – *What about the last meeting you had in English?* Encourage general discussion so you can formulate a set of needs for the whole group.

- Summarise what has been found out/agreed and make notes. Write up their main needs if you want to refer to them later (see *Course objectives meeting* on page 31).

Alternative Prepare a needs analysis interview questionnaire (page 30). Get the learners to work in pairs and interview their partner. Ask one from each pair to report on what their partner said. Encourage whole-group discussion so you can formulate a set of group needs.

Review Type up what was agreed during the lesson. Give this to the learners in the next lesson in the form of 'minutes'. Regularly refer to these throughout the course.

Open questions

Current/future use of English	Goals/priorities	Learning preferences
• Tell me about your job. • How often do you use English at work? • In what kind of situations do you use English? • What do you have to do in English? • When was the last time you used English? • Will you need English more in the future and, if so, in what situations? • When will the next time be? • Tell me about your last/next English meeting/telephone call/email/ negotiation/presentation/social event, etc.	• What would you like to focus on in these English lessons? • What do you think you already do well in English? • What would you like to be able to do better? • What do you find difficult about meetings/telephoning/presenting/ negotiating/emailing in English? • How will you know that you are better able to present/discuss/negotiate, etc, in English? • Tell me about your last meeting/ telephone call in English. What went well? What could have gone better?	• When you speak, do you want to be corrected immediately or at the end of the task? • How much time do you want to spend doing homework between lessons? • What homework activities do you find useful? • How will you review the information that we covered in the lessons? • Are you comfortable working in groups? • How did you learn vocabulary when you were at school? • How do you like learning – by reading and making notes/listening and making notes/memorising, etc?

Probing questions

Areas of concern	What you need to find out	Possible answers	Possible objectives
Speaking	What do you need to be able to speak about?	Jobs Products	To be able to talk about jobs and responsibilities/products
Reading	What do you need to be able to read?	Contracts Manuals	To be able to understand different types of work-related documents
Writing	What do you have to write in English? Who do you write it to? What do you write about?	Emails Colleagues in France Quality problems	To improve ability to write emails about work-related topics
Listening	In which situations do you have difficulty understanding spoken English? Do you mostly have contact with native or non-native speakers of English?	Taking part in tele-conferences Japanese colleagues	To improve understanding of native speakers and different accents
Vocabulary	What vocabulary areas would be useful for you? What other vocabulary topics would be interesting for you?	Finance Marketing Vocabulary to describe the products my company sells	To extend the range of vocabulary related to finance/marketing To extend the range of vocabulary to talk about products
Meetings	What do you find difficult about taking part in meetings?	Native speakers interrupt me all the time.	To extend the range of standard phrases for preventing interruptions
Presentations	What do you find difficult about presenting in English? What do you give presentations about?	I feel I am not as persuasive as I am in my own language. Company products	To extend the range of persuasive language To be able to give presentations about company products
Telephoning	What do you find difficult about telephoning in English? What do you telephone about?	Taking messages when native speakers call my boss	To be able to take phone messages from native speakers

Course objectives meeting

Principle Learners need to prioritise their course objectives. As it is impossible to meet everyone's needs, group members have to rank objectives and make compromises. Do a 'meetings' roleplay to help them to decide. A good follow-up to *English tick list* or *Needs analysis interview* (page 29).

Prepare

Make enough copies of an agenda for each learner. If you have written up their needs on the board/flipchart earlier in the lesson, leave them there so the learners can refer to them.

> **Meeting agenda**   Group: Date:
>
> **Aims:** • To discuss the group's English needs
> • To decide three or four course objectives
>
> 1 Welcome/introductions
> 2 Clarify aims of the meeting
> 3 Topics for discussion:
> • Typical situations where the group uses English
> • Areas in English the group would like to improve
> • What people expect to learn in this course
> • Decision on course objectives

Proceed

■ Tell the learners that they are going to take part in a meeting. The aim is to agree three or four objectives for the course which suit the whole group's needs.

■ Elicit what an example of an objective could be – *To learn phrases for participating in meetings and discussions.*

■ Hand out the agenda. Give everyone a few minutes to read it and think about what they are going to say, making notes if they want to and asking you any questions about the agenda or about ways of expressing themselves. Remind them to refer to their needs, if they are written up.

■ Appoint a chairperson and set a time limit for the 'meeting'.

■ During the meeting, monitor closely and make notes on *what* the learners say and also *how* they say it. This will give you ideas about vocabulary, grammar, pronunciation and functional language which you need to cover.

■ In the final stage, they should be able to give you three or four main objectives for the course, which you can use to plan the programme. You may need to ask 'probing questions' (page 30) to make the objectives more specific.

Follow-up Ask a learner to write up what was agreed in the meeting and to email it to all the other participants.

Review Do the meeting again after 8–10 lessons. Change the agenda: *What have we learned so far? What do we want to focus on next?*

Priority cards

Principle Learners need to have clear course objectives. Give extra support to discussions of needs and goals, and follow up with 'probing questions' so you get the information you want. A good follow-up to *English tick list* or *Needs analysis interview* (page 29).

Prepare

Put typical needs on index cards. There are some examples below – but for your learners there will be others. You will need one set for every three or four learners in the group.

Socialising	Writing emails	Work-related vocabulary
Speaking about work-related topics	Grammar	Meetings
Writing reports	General vocabulary	Speaking about general topics
Listening	Pronunciation	Telephoning

Proceed

■ Put the learners into groups of three or four and give out one set of cards per group. Explain that the aim of the activity is to decide on three or four main objectives for the course which suit the whole group's needs.

■ Tell the learners to choose four cards which are most important for *all* of them to focus on during the course.

■ While they discuss, monitor closely and make notes about *what* they say and *how* they say it – to give you ideas about vocabulary, grammar, pronunciation and functional language which you will need to cover.

■ At the end of the discussion, get the learners to tell you their main objectives, which you can use to plan your lessons. At this stage, ask probing questions to make the objectives more specific if necessary.

Alternative Instead of handing out all the cards, only give out the needs that the learners mentioned during the needs analysis activity.

Or provide blank cards – the learners write down key areas they want to focus on. Get them to pool the cards (on the board or a table) and sort them. Then guide the group to agree three or four key objectives for the course, asking them questions to find out exactly what is wanted in each area.

One-to-one Get the learner to order your cards from the *most* important to the *least* important.

Renewing needs

Principle Learners need to renew their motivation and their priorities if they have taken part in a previous course and decided to continue, perhaps after a break – or to stay motivated when courses continue over a long period and progress might be slow. Encourage them to reflect on what they have done in the past and what they want to focus on in the future.

Prepare

If you taught the learners before, take some time to go back through your notes, to remind yourself what you did previously and to reflect on what you feel they should focus on now. If you are taking over from another teacher, find out as much information as possible, either by talking to them or by going through the notes that they left.

Proceed

■ On the board/flipchart, write up the following:
  - In the previous course, we learned …
  - I am continuing because …
  - In this course, I would like to focus on …
  - By the end of the course, I hope to be able to …

■ Give the learners time to complete the sentences individually and then form small groups to discuss their answers. Set a time limit.

■ Monitor during the activity and make notes, gathering as much information as you can.

■ Ask the learners to report back on what their group discussed. Encourage general discussion so you can better formulate a set of collective needs.

■ Summarise what has been found out/agreed. Write down the learners' main needs, for future reference.

Alternative If the learners find it difficult to say what they want to focus on, you may want to use some of the 'probing questions' on page 30 to help them.

Review If the learners agreed course objectives in their previous lessons, get them to reflect on which ones they achieved and which ones they didn't. Elicit the reasons why, and use this information to get them to set new, perhaps more realistic targets.

Intensive aims

Principle Learners need to identify exactly the areas where they have made progress on an intensive course – huge advances are often made in just a week when they use English every day. To be able to analyse their progress together (and identify improvements and needs for further improvement) do this activity on the first day of the course.

Prepare

You need equipment for recording your learners – a voice recorder, an MP3 player with a recording function or a cassette recorder. Look at the learners' needs analysis (if you have one) and think of a realistic task for them to do – such as describing the responsibilities of their job or roleplaying a phone call.

Proceed

■ On the first day, explain the task:
  - You are going to record them doing the task but you are not going to listen to it until the end of the week so that you can see how much progress has been made.
  - This attempt does not have to be perfect – that's why they have chosen to do an English course!
  The learners do the task and you record it.

■ On the final day of the course, give the learners the task again and record them again. In what ways do they think this version is going be better than the first version? Consider specific things you have covered on the course, such as:
  - Grammar
  - Vocabulary
  - Pronunciation
  - Style (diplomatic language)

■ Play both versions and compare them. Focus specifically on the areas covered during the week.

■ Talk about what areas they would still like to improve after listening to the second version.

Alternative You can also video instead of just voice-recording, which would be especially appropriate for presentations.

Obviously, this activity can be done after the first week of a two-week course, for example, and you can proceed to concentrate on their *changed* needs.

I need to pass!

Principle Learners need to commit right from the start if they are preparing for an exam qualification. Help them to see how much work will be involved, both in lessons and in their own time, and motivate them by getting them to talk about their reasons for taking this exam.

Prepare
If you are teaching an exam-preparation course for the first time, make sure you take the time to familiarise *yourself* with the exam.

Proceed
■ On the board/flipchart, write up the following:
- I am taking part in an exam-preparation course because …
- The differences between an exam course and a general business English course are …
- I think the best way to prepare for the exam is …
- In lessons, I would like to prepare for the exam by …
- At home, I would like to prepare for the exam by …

■ Give the learners time to complete the sentences individually. Put them into small groups to discuss their answers. Set a time limit.

■ Monitor during the activity and make notes so you can gather as much information as possible. Also remember to listen out for *how* they say things, not only *what* they say.

■ Ask the learners to report back on what their group discussed. Encourage a general discussion about the exam:
- Explain that a business English course would focus on learners' specific work-related needs whereas in an exam-preparation course they should expect to spend time on exam technique and practice.
- Explain that the exam might include topics and skills they do not need – writing reports or giving presentations, for example. However, they need to be able to do these things in the exam so they need to master them.

■ Discuss how much time the learners have to do homework and what exercises they would find most useful. Do they want to do practice exams at home or in the lessons? Emphasise that if they do practice papers at home, more time can be spent in the lessons focusing on speaking.

■ Summarise what has been found out/agreed and write it down, to refer to in future lessons.

Follow-up Do *Exam questionnaire* (see opposite).

Exam questionnaire

Principle Learners, if they are seeking qualifications, need to know their 'way round' their exam and to know what to expect – so they don't waste precious time on the day working out what to do. Look into the examination format in the first lessons of the course.

Prepare
Write questions about the exam – good exam coursebooks will contain all the answers to these questions, often in an introduction or appendix.
- How many parts are there?
- How long does the reading test last?
- How many people will do the speaking test with them?
- What are the marking criteria for the writing test?

Make a copy of the questionnaire for each learner.

Proceed
■ Give out the questionnaires.

■ Give the learners a few minutes to read the questions and to write down any answers they already know or can guess.

■ They compare with a partner and discuss what they already know or *think* they know about the exam.

■ Direct them to the part of the coursebook or the exam guide where they can find the answers. Set a time limit.

■ Go through the questions together to check that everyone has the correct information. At this point, some learners may also want to ask further questions.

Alternative The discussion could be done in class, with the information search being set as homework. Start the next lesson by asking the learners to compare what they were able to find out.

Business professionals If they have taken part in general business English courses in the past, you may want to begin this activity by eliciting the differences between a general business English course and an exam-preparation course.

Be sure to insist that in an exam course more time will be spent on exam technique and exam practice and that they might have to develop skills that they do not necessarily need for their job. Then move on to the exam questionnaire.

Future needs

Principle Learners, especially those with no professional experience, need to be able to connect what they are going to learn in the classroom to their futures in the business world. Raise their awareness – Why do business professionals need English for their jobs? How will the course prepare them for their future careers?

Prepare

Find a picture of a famous business manager who all your learners will recognise, perhaps a CEO from a multi-national company. If you are teaching a heterogeneous group, then try to find pictures from a variety of cultures.

Proceed

■ Show the picture(s) to your learners and elicit information about the people.

■ Put the learners into groups and get them to make a list of what the manager has to be able to do in English for their job – take part in negotiations, lead meetings, understand complicated reports, etc. Set a time limit.

■ Collect the main ideas on the board/flipchart.

■ Ask the learners to discuss in their groups which of the tasks listed on the board they would be able to do *now* and which ones they would find *difficult*.

■ If your course objectives have already been set by your institution, refer to these – using the information you have collected – to decide how working towards the objectives will help the learners to become better future managers.

Alternative Instead of using pictures, write job titles such as 'Sales Manager' or 'Financial Director' on the board/flipchart. Put the learners into groups to brainstorm what managers in each of the various fields would have to be able to do in English if they had customers in other countries.

Or ask the whole group what types of jobs they imagine having in the future, and write these up. In small groups, they discuss how important English will be for these jobs, and how improving their English now will help them to prepare for their later careers.

Review At the end of the course, show the pictures of the manager again. Remind the learners what they said at the beginning of the course. Ask them what they would now find easier to do – now that the course is over.

A day in the life …

Principle Learners need to be able to talk confidently about their jobs. Give them practice in the first lessons – and learn a lot of useful information about their working life for when doing your course planning around job-related activities.

Prepare

Have ready a pack of blank index cards.

Proceed

■ Elicit on the board/flipchart three things the learners typically do in their jobs – write emails, greet visitors, take part in meetings, etc.

■ Put the learners into pairs and give each pair about ten index cards. Tell them to put on each card one thing they do in a normal day, using the models on the board as examples.

■ When all or most of the cards are written, nominate one person in each pair to be Learner A and the other to be Learner B.

    ● Learner A puts the cards in order, from the things they spend *most time* on to the things they spend *least time* on, then tell their partner about this.

    ● Learner B should then quickly say if their day is similar or different.

    ● Leaner B puts the cards in order, from the things which are *most important* in their job to the things which are *least important*, then tells A about this.

    ● Learner A should then quickly say if their priorities are similar or different.

■ Give the learners feedback, and summarise any useful language they need for talking about their jobs more accurately.

■ Keep a record of their priorities for your future planning.

Alternative After Learner A has spoken about the amount of time they spend on different tasks, get Learner B to report on what they have found out to the rest of the group. Do the same after Learner B talks about the most important tasks.

Follow-up After feedback, get the learners to write example sentences using the new language you give them.

One-to-one Get the learner to write on the cards, then do both ranking tasks, explaining to you what order they have decided, and why.

My job, my company

Principle Learners need to feel comfortable speaking English in the classroom. Get them out of their seats early in the course and presenting – an activity which is familiar to many of them in their jobs. This works especially well with one-to-one learners or with small groups.

Prepare
Find out as much as possible about the structure of the company that the learners work for. What is the name of the CEO? What divisions does the company have?

Proceed
■ Explain to the learners that they are going prepare a small presentation so that you can learn as much as possible about their job and their company. Write a sample organigram on the board/flipchart:

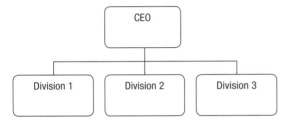

■ Elicit the name of the head of the company and write it up, then elicit the main divisions and write these up.

■ Hand the pen over to one of the learners. They complete the organisation chart so it includes their own job and clearly shows who they report to and who reports to them. Then elicit the same information from the rest of the group.

■ Get the learners to prepare a short presentation (3–5 minutes) about their job, including their main responsibilities and duties and those of their team. You may need to pre-teach phrases like 'report to' or 'be responsible for'.

■ When they are ready, they come up to the board and present their job, referring to the organisation chart as necessary. The rest of the group ask follow-up questions:
  - *Which parts of your job do you have to do in English?*
  - *Which duties take the most time?*
  - *Which ones can you delegate to your team members?*

Alternative Record the learners, either with audio or video. Play the recording and get them to evaluate themselves and each other, if you think it suitable.

Review During or at the end of the course, set the same task and record it again. The learners compare their performances – as a measurement of their progress.

My job, your job

Principle Learners need to be able to talk and ask questions about their own jobs and those of their business partners. Get them talking about what they do – and identify grammar areas (How well can they form questions and use tenses?) which need work during the course.

Prepare
Make sure the learners have a basic grasp of question formation. Perhaps do some review work before the activity.

Proceed
■ Elicit typical daily tasks on the board. This could take the form of a list or a mindmap. You can also get one of the learners to come and write tasks on the board with the help of the rest of the group.

■ Put the learners into pairs and tell each pair to write six questions, using the tasks on the board as prompts. These should be questions which will enable them to find out more about each other's working days. Both learners in the pair need to write the questions down.

■ Monitor while they are writing, to check the questions are correct.

■ Once each learner has their six questions, get them to work with a new partner. Set a time limit to ask and answer the questions. Encourage them to ask follow-up questions to find out more information.

■ This stage can be followed by another pairing, so they can ask their questions to a second person – if time allows.

■ Give feedback and summarise any useful language needed for talking about jobs more accurately.

Higher levels Give a model – *How often do you have meetings?* – then let the learners write the rest of the questions individually.

Review If you want to revisit language areas, you can do the following:

Focus on tenses by asking the learners to write at least two questions which refer to the past – *When was your last meeting?* And two which refer to the future – *Where are you going on your next business trip?*

Focus on adjectives – *When was your last useful meeting?* Or conditionals – *What would you do if …?*

Focus on comparisons by giving prompts such as *What is your favourite …? When was the best/most successful, most interesting, worst X you have ever (been to, taken part in …)? Do you prefer X or Y?*

My new boss

Principle Learners need to be able to be able introduce themselves in multinational situations. Get them to practise realistic roleplays at the very beginning of the course – simulations will be a frequent activity and they need to be made to feel comfortable as soon as possible.

Prepare

Prepare a handout with phrases that the learners can use when talking about their jobs. This can include phrases such as *I report to …* or *My main responsibilities include … .* Most business English coursebooks include such phrases.

Proceed

■ Tell the learners to imagine that they are about to attend an international meeting and that they will need to introduce themselves in English. Elicit the information that they would typically include in such an introduction – their main responsibilities, who they report to, etc. Write these on the board/flipchart.

■ Tell them that their company has a new CEO who has organised a meeting to get to know staff members. This new CEO does not speak the local language, so the meeting will be held in English. They all have to prepare a short presentation of their jobs.

■ Give them the handout with the useful phrases and some time to prepare their introductions.

■ Put them into small groups to practise. Group members should give each other feedback on how their presentations could be improved. After this, give them some time to make changes.

■ Take the role of the new CEO yourself. Leave the room, come back in and shake the learners' hands – you are meeting them for the first time.

■ Invite them to introduce themselves and their jobs, asking them questions to get more information about their main responsibilities and tasks.

■ Summarise any useful language they need for talking about their jobs more accurately.

■ Get the learners to add the new language from the feedback to their notes on their real presentations for future reference.

Alternative Ask one of the learners to take on the role of the CEO. This way, you can pay more attention to the language that they are all using, as opposed to the content.

Nobody's perfect

Principle Learners need to be made aware of their mistakes to make progress. However, not everyone may feel comfortable having their mistakes pointed out in the first lessons. Instead, give them a list of common errors – go through the list and discuss how the learners want to be corrected. This is a good follow-up to getting them to talk about their jobs (see *My job, my company* and *My job, your job* on page 35).

Prepare

Make a list of common errors that learners make when talking about their jobs. For example:
- Saying *My job involves to take care of customers*
- Calling the boss their *chef*
- Mispronouncing *Chief Executive Officer*

If you are new to the field of business English teaching or to the country you are in, you may want to ask a more experienced teacher to help you come up with a comprehensive list.

Proceed

■ After getting the learners to talk about their jobs, elicit what is meant by a 'common mistake'. Point out that mistakes can be very varied:
- Grammar or vocabulary
- Pronunciation
- Formal/informal language used inappropriately
- First-language interference

■ Spend some time talking about typical mistakes and how they are not necessarily negative – you *learn* from them.

■ Give out your list of common errors. Put the learners into small groups and get them to correct the mistakes.

■ During feedback, discuss how they would like you to handle error-correction in your lessons:
- Should you correct immediately?
- Should you write things down and correct later?

■ Encourage the learners to prioritise their mistakes and to choose two or three that they would like to focus on during the course.

Review Get the learners to choose two or three common errors and write them down on an index card. Encourage them to refer to their cards at the beginning of every lesson and to focus on getting them right.

Independence day

Principle Learners need strategies for reviewing and recording vocabulary on their own, strategies which are easy to work with, motivating and effective. Encourage them to be independent from day one and record vocabulary systematically.

Prepare

Make a 'card sort' with company-related vocabulary like the examples opposite. Half the set of cards will have work-related words, and the other half the definitions of the words in English (use a monolingual dictionary to help you). Prepare one complete set for every three to four learners. Depending on their level, choose suitable words.

Also prepare a checklist for yourself of different strategies for recording vocabulary (see opposite too).

Proceed

- Put the learners into small groups and give each group a complete set of cards. Ask them to match the words with the correct definitions.

- Check that the match is correct. Ask them which vocabulary is new and which they would like to learn.

- Get ideas of how they might learn these words:
  - What did they do at school or on previous language courses?
  - How do they learn things in other situations – new tasks for their job?

- Elicit options for recording new vocabulary, and discuss strategies like those opposite.

- Discuss ways of keeping a record – Index cards? A ring-binder? What are the advantages/disadvantages?
  - Index cards are easier to sort – words I know, words I nearly know, words I don't know at all …
  - Ring-binders are easier to sort into sections – vocabulary connected with my job, phrases for presentations …

Higher levels Get the learners to practise the words by preparing, and then giving, a presentation of their company.

Lower levels Get them to write sentences about their company or a company that they know well.

Pronunciation Get them to use monolingual (or online) dictionaries to record the pronunciation of the words. You can do a follow-up session on learner dictionaries, to demonstrate the amount of useful information they contain – especially features such as pronunciation and example sentences.

Learner cards

subsidary	Definition
headquarters	Definition
to found	Definition
to manufacture	Definition

Learner strategies

English definitions

- They can revisit the definitions cards only, and see if they can remember the words. And vice-versa.
- If they read a word they want to remember in an article, they can write out the whole sentence or get a definition sentence from a monolingual dictionary.

Word families

- They look at the words on their cards and find word families for them.
- They record the nouns of the verbs:
  To employ – *employee/employer/employment*
  To compete – *competitor/competition*
- They record other parts of speech:
  Employed – *unemployed*
  Competitive – *competing*

Word partnerships

- They record words that can make a partnership:
  Business – in business, a small business, business card, business studies
- They look at the words on the cards and think of word partnerships for them, paying special attention to whether the accompanying word goes before or after:
  Company + headquarters / policy / culture
  Market-driven / cutting-edge / progressive + company
- They use the example sentences in a monolingual dictionary to check on useful word partnerships.
- They use an online concordance program to check on frequent partnerships.

Review cards

Principle Learners need to review language regularly to turn input into learning – in lessons, in their jobs and in their own reading or listening to English. Do this activity two or three lessons into the course, in order to review language covered so far and to give strategies for reviewing. It works especially well with one-to-one learners but can also work with groups.

Prepare

You will need four or five index cards. Look back at your notes from the first lessons. Make sample cards like those opposite, based on new language that came up.

Proceed

- Ask the learners if they have reviewed new language from previous lessons and, if so, how they reviewed it.
- Tell them that you want to show them a system for recording new language that many learners find useful.
- Take out the sample cards that you prepared:
  - Show the learners the front of the card.
  - Elicit the answer on the back.
- Sum up by discussing the advantages of using cards. See the box opposite for some examples.

Index cards If the learners like the idea of working with cards, then always bring a few to the lessons. They record new language directly onto the cards during the lessons.

Binders If the learners are hesitant to use cards, suggest using ring-binders. They keep a list of 'typical mistakes' and a section for recording 'vocabulary' at the front of the file, to refer to easily. Language for 'business skills', such as negotiations, could be kept in another section.

Computerised cards Another alternative is they create a 'paperless card box' on their computers. They can immediately record language that they want to learn into their laptops and then review it in the office or on business trips.

Card review box Before each lesson, make a few cards for reviewing what you did in the previous lesson. Put in the 'card review box'. The learners take turns 'quizzing' each other at the beginning of the lesson while they are waiting for everyone to arrive.

Reviewing language

Card 1 (front)	(back)
Phrases for describing my job …	My job involves … My main duties include … I report to …

Card 2 (front)	(back)
Typical mistake *My job involves to talk to customers.*	My job involves talking to customers.

Card 3 (front)	(back)
Two companies that produce and sell the same products in the same market	*Competitors* (*to compete* – verb)

Using cards

- They are easy to transport – so they can be taken on business trips.
- They are flexible – you can move cards you are familiar with to the back of the box but keep cards you still need to review nearer the front.
- They are good for learners who like to 'do things' to help them remember – putting the cards in piles, moving them around.
- They are good for learners to test themselves – by looking at one side and trying to remember what is on the other.
- It is easy to choose a small number – eg three cards – as a target to learn each day.
- It can be time-consuming to make the cards – but writing them out by hand and thinking about what to add can make things easier to remember.

Personal action plan

Principle Learners need to increase their exposure to English outside the classroom wherever possible. This is important for those on an on-going course, so they can make the most of the time between lessons. Also on intensive courses, so they can consolidate what they have learned and keep making progress after the course has finished.

Prepare
Make a copy of the 'Personal action plan' below for each learner in the group.

Proceed
- Write 'Things to try in English' in the middle of the board/flipchart. Give an example which you know some people in the group already do or might be interested in – watch films in English or read the international trade press.

- Ask the learners for more ideas, and write them up as a mindmap. Cover all the skills (listening, reading, writing and speaking) and make suggestions yourself.

- Once the board is full, give out the personal action plans. Ask the learners to choose one or two things from the board they would like to try, and add them to the first boxes of their plan with a date – *I will buy and read a graded reader by the end of next month*. Get them to write down what they need to do to achieve the aim – *Join the library so that I can borrow a graded reader*.

- Put them into pairs to compare their plans.

- Get feedback from the whole group. Record in your file what they plan to do – to remind them regularly throughout the course.

Alternative Instead of just listing ideas, show actual examples of websites, graded readers, magazines, books, etc, that you think the learners will find useful. Give them time to look at and try out the material.

They can be given one resource to 'present' to the rest of the group. What might they find possible in the time they have available and at their level of English? When could they use the materials – listening to podcasts/audio books on the way to work, or watching DVDs on the plane on their way to a business meeting?

Lower levels Extra guidance will be needed – suggest that the learners watch DVDs with subtitles, or watch first in their own language then again in English (or even just a small part). Make them aware of lower-level graded readers and other elementary resources on the internet.

They can also write their action plans in their own language if they prefer.

Review Refer back to the action plans throughout the course and get the learners to fill up more boxes with new strategies for increasing their contact with English.

Things I will try to do in English:	Date I will do this by:	What I need to do:
Examples: *Read a novel* *Do grammar exercises on the internet*	Examples: *The end of the year* *This weekend*	Examples: *Join the library* *Get suggestions of good internet sites*
1		
2		
3		
4		

Watching the web

Principle Learners need guidance on how they can use the internet to help them learn English. Although this is a familiar resource, available for most people, provide initial classroom support – because the sheer amount of information can make it a daunting task to begin.

Prepare

Before the lesson, spend time on the internet looking at sites for learning English. For the lesson, you will need a computer with internet access for each individual or pair.

Proceed

- Elicit websites the learners already know which are specifically for people learning English.
  - Have they tried any?
  - What did they think of them?
- Set a time limit – perhaps 30 minutes – to find and try out some good websites for learning English. The learners should be prepared to report back to the group on their favourites. If they use a search engine and type in 'learning English', they ought to find plenty.
- After the time limit, get them to share their experiences and recommendations.

Alternative If you don't have access to computers with internet, make a list of your 'top five' internet sites for learning English. Give out the list and assign each learner a site to investigate. They should report back in the next lesson. This could be in the form of a short presentation or written summary/report, depending on *your* objectives and *their* needs.

One-to-one Look through the internet together, to demonstrate how easy it is to find good websites, then set the task of looking at the internet sites as a homework assignment and reporting back during next lesson.

Personal plans If the learners would find it useful to use the internet to learn English and if they want to experiment on their own at home, get them to write it down on their 'personal action plan'. Record this in your own file so that you remember to ask them in the near future if they tried it out and how it went.

Yesterday's news

Principle Learners need strategies for improving their listening skills, and a natural way of doing this is by watching the news. Give them a 'framework' to focus on and facilitate comprehension – their background knowledge of topical news items should give them support in understanding.

Prepare

Record three to five minutes of the news in English the day before the lesson. The headlines or a short bulletin before a main programme work well. Watch it yourself and write down the main events that are discussed.

Proceed

- Tell the learners that they are going to watch yesterday's news in English.
- Put them into small groups and ask them to think of five events that they expect to be discussed in the news. They should base this on what they have seen or read in the news in their own language.
- Elicit ideas and write up the contributions.
- Tell them that when they watch the news, they only have to listen for the items you have listed.
- Play the recording and elicit which of the items on the board were discussed.

Follow-up Get the learners to ask each other questions about the news events – their opinion about a specific politician, etc.

Podcasts If you do not have facilities to play a video or DVD, use a news podcast from the internet.

Personal plans If the learners want to practise listening on their own at home, get them to write this down on their 'personal action plan'. Record it also in your own file so that you remember to ask them in the near future – Did they try it out? How did it go?

Explain that they can take two minutes to think about what events they expect to see and then check if they are correct. If they have already read or watched the news in their own language, they should already be familiar with the content and therefore should not feel overwhelmed by new vocabulary or the speed of the presenters' delivery.

Dictionary quiz

Principle Learners need to be able to use learner dictionaries, both in lessons and in their offices. Get them acquainted with the basic layout and terminology of monolingual dictionaries so that it is easier for them to work on their own.

Prepare

Write a quiz, or use the one opposite, and make a copy for every learner in the group. Make a copy of one entry for one word on an OHT. Use one of the words from the quiz – eg *subsidiary*. Provide a learner dictionary for every two or three learners.

Proceed

■ Put the learners into groups of two or three, and give each group a dictionary.

■ Spend time familiarising the learners with dictionary layouts and terminology:
  - What terminology is used?
  - What does (adj) mean?
  - What does (n) mean?
  - What does (v) mean?

■ Ask the learners what information they expect to find about a word in the dictionary. Show them the entry that you have prepared on the OHT and elicit what information is included. Point out the terminology and other features – stress markers – which are useful for completing the quiz.

■ Give out copies of the quiz. Get the learners to complete it, using the dictionary.

Alternative If the learners are resistant to using monolingual dictionaries, you can compare them to bilingual dictionaries:
  - Give half the group bilingual dictionaries and the other half learner dictionaries.
  - Ask the two groups to complete the quiz and then compare their answers.
  - Get them to reflect on what information is missing in the bilingual dictionaries.

If teaching in a room with internet access, get half the groups to use an online monolingual dictionary and the other half an online bilingual dictionary.

Learner autonomy Encourage the use of learner dictionaries to keep records of stress patterns, sample sentences, grammatical information, etc.

---

1 What does '**fluctuation**' mean? Circle the correct answer:

A *Continuous changes, especially from one level to another – eg changes in price*

B *A statistic about how many people have left a company*

C *Both*

2 What are the nouns of the following verbs?

Verb	Noun
to subsidise	
to endorse	
to propose	

3 Underline the stressed syllable for the nouns below:

executive

hierarchy

subsidiary

4 '**Actual**' and '**current**' are words that are sometimes confused. Complete the sentences below with the correct word:

We thought that we would sell 30,000 units but the _____ sales number was much higher.

Our most _____ product is the X34-S.

5 Complete the sentences below with the correct preposition:

He was blamed _____ the mistake.

She gave a really good recommendation _____ how to solve the problem.

Words under stress

Principle Learners need to use correct intonation when speaking. Business English learners often have a passive range of work-related vocabulary but have difficulty pronouncing the words. At best, using incorrect word stress can make the learner sound unprofessional and put strain on the listener. At worst, it can lead to misunderstanding or breakdown in communication. Use monolingual dictionaries to introduce word stress patterns – even with elementary learners.

Prepare

Make a set of cards. Half the cards have pictures of different jobs, and the other half contain the names of the jobs – *pilot, mechanic, police officer, businessperson, factory worker* or *laboratory technician*. Make a complete set of cards and provide a monolingual dictionary or access to a monolingual dictionary website for every two or three learners.

Before the lesson begins, write up the words on the board/flipchart.

Proceed

- Give out the sets of cards and ask the learners to match the jobs with the pictures.
- Point out the spelling of one of the words on the board and ask the learners which syllable is stressed. Get them to check by looking in the dictionary.
  - They work in pairs and find out which syllables are stressed in the other words.
  - They take it in turns to come up to the board and write a large dot over the stressed syllables.
- They can record the stress patterns in their vocabulary notebooks or on their vocabulary cards.

Alternative Divide the class into teams. Say the definition of one of the words and ask one team to say the word. The team gets a point if they pronounce the word correctly. Repeat the procedure for each team and keep track of the points. The team with the most points wins.

Review Make a note of incorrect use of word stress patterns during your lessons. Write these words on the board and get the learners to use learner dictionaries to find the correct word stress.

Learner autonomy Get them to underline key words in their own presentations and to use learner dictionaries to check that they have the correct stress patterns. Encourage them to go to online dictionaries and listen to the pronunciation of the words – to be sure.

Candidate case study

Principle Learners need to see the direct benefits of using dictionaries for their jobs. Do a realistic task – deciding between candidates for a job – and work on word formation.

Prepare

Make a list of adjectives to describe people's character:

calm	*friendly*
confident	*practical*
creative	*relaxed*
dependable	*reliable*

Write a job advertisement or use an authentic advert from the company's website or elsewhere on the internet.

Write profiles or CVs for three people who might apply for the job advertised, giving such details as age, previous work experience and qualifications. Make copies for each learner, with the advert and the candidate profiles on separate sheets.

Provide a learner dictionary for every two or three learners.

Proceed

- Write the following columns on the board:

  Adjective   Noun

- Elicit the meaning of the word 'reliable'. Ask the learners to find the noun of 'reliable'. Monitor and help, as necessary. They copy the chart on a piece of paper, adding 'reliability'.
- Show the entry for 'reliable'. Point out how learner dictionaries give information on word formation and word stress.
- Dictate the other adjectives, giving time to write them down in the 'Adjective' column. The learners then write the nouns and mark the word stress.
- In groups, give them the advert to read.
- Write on the board:
  - *The ideal candidate should be …*
  - *… is important for this job.*
- With their partners, they complete the sentences, using words from the list. Monitor, and check the pronunciation.
- Give out the candidates' descriptions and give the learners time to decide who would be most suited for the job.

Follow-up For additional speaking practice, the learners discuss their jobs and the importance of the various qualities – *creativity played a big part in my previous job*, etc.

Review During fluency activities, write down business words the learners use. During feedback, elicit the word families. If they don't know them, they look them up in a dictionary.

Multi-word verb search

Principle Learners need to understand and practise multi-word verbs: verbs plus one – or sometimes more than one – preposition (*They put off the meeting until the following week*) or adverb (*The negotiations broke down*). These are very common in business English, but learners often use more formal equivalents (*They postponed the meeting*). Show them how monolingual dictionaries can help.

Prepare
Prepare a list of work-related multi-word verbs and their definitions. Make sure the verbs are defined in the dictionary that you have chosen and provide a dictionary for every two or three learners.

Use the multi-word verbs and the definitions to prepare a card-matching activity, and make one complete set of cards for every two or three learners.

Proceed
- Tell the learners that they are going to focus on multi-word verbs (in this activity we are using verbs with prepositions). To check that they know what these are, elicit some examples.
- Put the learners into groups. Give each group Set A and Set B of the cards. Ask them to match the verbs with prepositions to form multi-word verbs. Set a time limit.
- Elicit what verbs they came up with and write them on the board, or give the pen to a learner to write them up.
- Give each group a learner dictionary. Ask them to check the definition of *one* of the multi-word verbs. Point out that dictionaries can help them to understand the meaning.
- Give each group Set C. Get them to match the verbs with the prepositions, in such a way that they match up with a definition. Encourage the use of the learner dictionaries to help.

Follow-up For additional writing practice, give the learners an email that has a great many examples of multi-word verbs (*put off*). Get them to rewrite it using more formal vocabulary (*postpone*).

Qualification seekers Follow up by giving them a text with the prepositions removed. Get them to put them back in. Elicit which prepositions are part of multi-word verbs. Remind the learners that business English exams often test multi-word verbs, so they have to be familiar with them if they want to succeed in the exam.

Review In the next lesson, give out Set C cards to the learners. Get each learner to take turns reading out the definition on their cards. The first person to say the correct multi-word verb gets a point. Continue until all the definitions have been read out – and declare a winner.

Card set A

put	cut	count
turn	lay	draw

Card set B

off	down	on
down	off	up

Card set C

To decide to delay an activity to a later time	To reduce	To rely on someone
To say 'no' to an offer	To make employees redundant	To write an official document, eg a contract

Guess the definition

Principle Learners need to be able to look up idioms which they may come across, especially if they deal with native speakers – idioms can be difficult as the meaning is not clear from the individual words. Use a dictionary to work out the meaning and teach a very useful skill.

Prepare
Make a list of business idioms. Preferably, select ones that are linked in some way – 'negotiations' – and make sure that they are defined in the dictionary that you have chosen. Provide a learner dictionary for every two or three learners.

Proceed
■ Write your list of idioms on the board:
> *To take a back seat*
> *To play your cards close to your chest*
> *To lay your cards on the table*

■ Choose one of the idioms and ask if anyone can tell you what it means. Encourage guesses.

■ Put the learners into small groups or pairs – you are going to give three definitions of the idiom, but only one is correct. They have to decide which.

■ Read out the real definition and two others. For example, if your idiom is '*to take a back seat*', the definitions could be:
> A To let someone else do the work
> B To steal something that nobody needs
> C To be given a worse job than the one you have

■ Ask the learners to discuss which they think is the correct answer. Repeat the definitions, if necessary.

■ Get the learners to find the meaning of the idiom in the dictionary. Suggest they look up the key words first (usually nouns and verbs).

■ Assign three idioms to each group of learners. They should use their dictionaries to write one *real* definition and three *fake* ones. Set a time limit. Monitor and help.

■ Get the groups to take it in turns to read out their idioms and definitions for the rest to guess.

Alternative Give out points for the right guesses, with a prize for the winner.

Homework Get the learners to read an authentic text from the internet. Tell them to find one or two idioms in the text and to use their learner dictionaries to figure out the definitions. In the next lesson, they should share them.

Idioms dictionaries In a subsequent lesson, introduce learners to dictionaries of idioms (online and hard copy) as another useful reference tool.

Revision quiz

Principle Learners need to sort out their notes, folders or files regularly. As the course progresses, they tend to collect more and more handouts and notes but often don't look through them. Help them to revise with a quiz – and get them to reflect on what they have learned.

Prepare
Make a copy of several model questions based on recent lessons for every two or three learners in the group. The questions should take different forms:
- Vocabulary you did in the course:
  Another word for 'cutting-edge' is …
- Grammar:
  Write down ten irregular 2nd forms (past simple)
- Content questions based on a text:
  Where did Bob Smith work for two years?
- Questions based on course content:
  What is a SWOT analysis?
  What are the stages of a negotiation?

Prior to the lesson, ask the learners to bring their course notes, to be able to refer to them.

Proceed
■ Put the learners into pairs and give them the quiz questions. Get them to look back through their course notes to find the answers.

■ Tell them to think of ten similar questions with their partner. The answers should be found in their course notes. They write out the questions (without the answers) on a piece of paper. Set a time limit.

■ When the time is up or the questions are complete, get the pairs to exchange with another pair. Get them to look through their notes to find the answers.

Alternative Get the learners to prepare their quizzes as homework and use them in the following lesson.

Lower levels Give some question prompts to help, and limit to only five questions.

Review Get the learners to revise the course content by preparing short presentations on what they have learned in the lessons so far.

Guess the word

Principle Learners need to be able to describe the meanings of words. This skill is crucial if they are in a meeting or on the telephone and cannot think of the exact word. It is also helpful if they are speaking to someone whose English is not as good as theirs and who may not understand something. Play a game where they practise this, while reviewing vocabulary that has been covered on the course.

Prepare

You need a pile of blank index cards. Also, ask the learners to bring their course notes, to be able to refer to them.

Proceed

- Give out several cards to the learners, individually or in pairs. Ask them to look through their notes from recent lessons and find some items of vocabulary they would still like to learn. They should write the words clearly on one side of the cards.

- Collect all the cards and shuffle them. Deal them out so that each pair of learners has a random selection.

- Get one learner from each pair to pick a card from their pile, look at it but not show it to their partner.
    - They give a definition or example sentence of the word until their partner guesses the word or gives up. Obviously, the definition or example sentence must not include the word on the card.
    - Their partner then has a turn, and so on until all the cards are gone (at which point they can exchange their pile with another pair and carry on).

- It does not matter too much if some of the words on the cards are the same, as these will probably be ones the learners consider most important so should be revised more frequently.

Follow-up Do *Half-and-half crossword* (see opposite).

Lower levels Limit the number of cards.

Qualification seekers Prepare vocabulary from the exam syllabus, or that causes problems in practice tests.

Review Collect the cards at the end of the activity and use them again in future lessons for further revision activities.

Learner autonomy Get them to write down definitions or example sentences for the words they did not know/ remember, for on-going revision, too. Encourage them to use cards to learn vocabulary on a regular basis.

Half-and-half crossword

Principle Learners need to revisit vocabulary constantly so that they can use it actively. Get them not only to review vocabulary but work on definitions and spelling, which they need for written communication.

Prepare

Choose a list of words from recent lessons you want to revise. (If you have made cards in *Guess the word* – see opposite – you can use these.) Put the words into a crossword. There are many websites which will do this for you – use an internet search engine to find one – and special software is also available.

Make two copies of the crossword with the 'answers' – all the words filled in. Label one 'Crossword A' and white out all the answers going *down*. Label the second 'Crossword B' and white out all the answers going *across*. You now have two different versions, one containing all the *down* answers and one containing all the *across* answers.

Make a copy of one or other of the crosswords for each learner in the group.

Proceed

- Put the learners into pairs and give one of the pair Version A and the other Version B. They must not show them to each other.
    - They take it in turns to ask their partner for definitions of the words – *What is 3 down?*
    - If they don't know the word, they can leave it and come back to it later when they have some more letters from other words.

- Continue until both learners have filled in all their words, or until they are stuck.

- At the end, get them to compare their crosswords and check that all the words are spelled correctly.

Lower levels Give the learners time to prepare definitions and write them down. They can do this individually or with others who have the same version of the crossword. Dictionaries could be used. The learners then do the activity – working in pairs and taking it in turns to ask their partner for definitions.

One-to-one Work as the learner's partner and provide the definitions.

Homework Get the learners to prepare their own crossword with clues. Collect these during the next lesson and use them later as a review in future lessons.

Business board game

Principle Learners need to be constantly reminded of typical errors so that they start to self-correct. However, this can become frustrating as they may begin to feel that they are not making progress. Play a game that enables them to review common mistakes in a relaxed atmosphere.

Prepare
Review some 'Feedback sheets' or your notes on common errors and make a copy of a game board for every four learners.

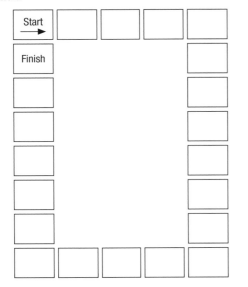

Write a sentence in each box from your notes – *I work here since three years.*

You will also need a dice for each game and counters for each learner.

Proceed
- Get the learners to put their counter on 'Start'.
- Get the first player to roll the dice and move their counter round the board for the number of squares they rolled.
- The learner reads the 'wrong' sentence and gives a 'right' version. If they are correct, they roll again and move again. If they give the wrong 'correction', they stay where they are and the next player takes a turn.
- The first player to reach 'Finish' is the winner.

Alternative Get the learners to write down example sentences, using the correct versions, as they play the game.

Homework Ask the learners to review the feedback sheets or notes in their files and make their own board game to play in a future lesson.

Business dictogloss

Principle Learners need to be aware of where they make grammatical errors, especially when writing. Enable them to review the grammar you have covered so far and to realise where they are still making errors.

Prepare
Find a copy of a business article you read in a previous lesson. Choose part of the article that includes grammatical structures that you have covered on the course.

Proceed
- Put the learners into pairs – *What do they remember about the text they read last lesson?* They discuss with their partner for a couple of minutes.
- Read a paragraph clearly but at normal speed. The learners then work with their partner and tell each other what they can remember.
- Explain you are going to read the paragraph again. This time they can take notes. However, as you are going to read it at the same speed, they won't be able to write everything down – it will be too fast.
  - They should concentrate on the content words – nouns and verbs – as they will be able to add the other words later.
  - If they miss part, they should just leave a space and carry on with the paragraph. As they are working as a pair, their partner might have heard the part they missed.
- Read the paragraph again – clearly but at normal speed. The learners write down as much as they can.
- They reconstruct the paragraph with their partner. Their text does not have to be exactly what you said, although it should be as close as possible and make sense both in content and grammar.
- When they have the paragraph written down, choose one person to come to the board. With the help of the whole group, they write up the paragraph. There will be differences of opinion, so some negotiating will be necessary.
- When the paragraph is on the board and everyone is happy, get the learners to check it against the original to see how close they were.
- Elicit ideas – *What do they need to follow up in future lessons?* – on tenses, article use, prepositional phrases, etc.

Alternative Instead of an article, use a business letter or a report.

Red light, green light

Principle Learners need to re-establish their course objectives mid-course. Show them where they have made progress and where they need to continue. The terms 'red light' and 'green light' are often used, especially in project management – *red light* means that a phase of a project is finished; *green light* that it is still continuing.

Prepare

Go through your notes to remind yourself of the content of the lessons so far. You will also need a red and a green marker. Write the main points on a flipchart. It can look like this:

Presentations	Language for signposting
	Key vocabulary for presentations
Vocabulary	Words for talking about my job
	Financial vocabulary
Grammar	Present perfect
	Past simple

Proceed

- At the start of the lesson, remind the learners of the course objectives. Display the flipchart to remind them what has been covered during the course to achieve these objectives. Then do a variety of review activities.

- At the end of the lesson, tell the learners that you want them to reflect on their progress. For each item on the flipchart, they should decide if it is 'red light' or 'green light'.
  - Red light means that they feel that they have learned the item.
  - Green light means that they want to continue with it during the next block of lessons.

- Put them into groups to discuss which items are which.

- Based on learner feedback, put either a green dot or a red dot next to each item. Use this information to prioritise the content for the next block of lessons.

Alternative Get the learners to brainstorm the content of the course under headings themselves.

Follow-up Do *Course objectives meeting* or *Priority cards* (page 31) to get the learners to re-prioritise their goals.

Learner autonomy If they feel that they haven't made progress in a specific area – Why? It may be necessary to give them strategies for reviewing English on their own and for increasing their contact with English. This is an opportunity to bring in the 'Personal action plan' (page 39) – to give them more responsibility for their own learning.

Review Save the flipchart so that you can use it again during the next review lesson or during the last lesson of the course, to get the learners to reflect once again on their progress.

How did it go?

Principle Learners need to review their course objectives and to reflect how far these were fulfilled. Hold a 'meeting' – and review the language of meetings at the same time.

Prepare

Prior to the lesson, you might want to ask the learners to review 'meetings' language or bring their notes, to be able to refer to them.

Make copies of an agenda for your lesson meeting.

Date:
Time:
Venue:
Agenda
1 Apologies
2 Matters arising
3 Course objectives
4 AOB

Proceed

- Explain that the lesson is a review of the course objectives through a meeting. The learners need to agree:
  - Which course objectives were fulfilled?
  - Which were not?
  - Why?

- Give each learner a copy of the agenda, as well as time to read it and prepare their ideas. Encourage them to review their notes for the language of meetings, if you wish.

- Elect a chairperson, remind the learners of the task and set a time limit.

- Get them to roleplay the meeting. Make notes about their performance and their comments.

- Discuss their comments.

One-to-one Do the meeting with the learner, in the form of an appraisal: they are the appraisee.

Follow-up Do *Summing it up* and *To be continued …* (see page 48).

Summing it up

Principle Learners need the chance to look back over the course and to review what they have covered. Surprise them with the amount of things they have done and help them to remember it all – and at the same time practise their speaking and presenting skills.

Prepare

Before the lesson, review your notes of the course and make a mindmap of what you have covered. Ask the learners to bring their notes on the language of presentations, and perhaps their general course notes.

Proceed

■ Explain that this lesson is an opportunity to reflect on the content of the course and that the learners are going to make a group presentation.

■ Get them to review their notes on presentations language, including phrases for handing over to another speaker.

■ Put 'Our course' in a circle in the middle of the board and write in each corner one of the four following headings: Vocabulary, Grammar, Business skills, Language skills.

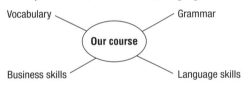

• Elicit examples under the headings 'Vocabulary' and 'Grammar'.
• Elicit subheadings for 'Business skills': *Presentations, Socialising*, etc.
• Elicit subheadings for 'Language skills': *Listening, Reading*, etc.

■ Put the learners into small groups. Give each group a piece of flipchart paper. Get them to copy the diagram and brainstorm what they remember from the course. They can go through their course notes if necessary.

■ Get the learners to divide up the presentation so each member of the group speaks. Set a time limit for the learners to prepare their section.

■ Finally, get each group to deliver their presentation. The other groups ask questions or give each other feedback.

Alternative The learners can make PowerPoint slides instead of using flipchart paper.

One-to-one Record the presentations and get the learner to do self-evaluation.

Personal plans Get the learners to summarise the successes of their personal action plans (page 39).

To be continued ...

Principle Learners need to spend time considering ways in which they can continue to learn English when a course finishes. Set an action plan with goals for future learning.

Prepare

Before the lesson, review your notes of the action plans the learners wrote in *Personal action plan* (page 39) so you can give prompts if necessary. Also, perhaps ask them to bring their personal plans to the lesson.

Have ready blank index cards and envelopes, one of each for every learner in the group.

Proceed

■ Get the learners to read through their action plans and/or to think of strategies they have learned on the course.

■ In pairs, they discuss which activities and strategies went well, and why. The pairs join another pair to share ideas.

■ Ask the learners to reflect: Which activities will they realistically continue on their own – after the course?

■ Give out the blank index cards. The learners individually write a list of three to five activities they want to do over the next three months.

■ Elicit what was covered during the course – grammar items and vocabulary topics. Write these on the board.

■ Ask the learners to reflect:
  • What language do they feel that they have learned?
  • What language do they need to review so it becomes more active?

■ Ask them to choose one or two things from the board that they feel they need to review, and a date by when they will review it. They write this on the cards too.

■ Give out the envelopes. The learners write their office address, put their index card inside and seal the envelope.

■ Collect the envelopes. Send them to the learners three months after the end of the course.

Personal action Give the learners new personal action plans and get them to add new goals and new dates.

Group action One of the action points could be to email each other after a period of time (or regularly) to say how they are getting on. This gives practice in writing English and also motivation to keep up with their plans.

One-to-one Email the learner or phone them after a month.

Lower levels Offer extra guidance – they could watch DVDs with subtitles or watch a film (or a part of it) first in their own language then in English. Remind them there are elementary graded readers, and elementary resources on the internet.

Chapter 2
The language of business

- Telephoning
- Emailing
- Presentations
- Meetings and discussions
- Negotiating
- Socialising

Telephoning

What do learners find difficult? There are many factors which make telephone calls more difficult than a face-to-face conversation:

- No visual support – facial expressions or gestures – to compensate for any language the learners lack. This makes it more important to understand what the speaker is saying, making listening for detail crucial.
- The unexpected nature of receiving phone calls gives learners no time to prepare and they may not know who is on the line before they answer.
- Conference calls involve three or more speakers and are a kind of meeting – so strategies for dealing with meetings can be applied. Telephone conferences should follow strict rules, to prevent everyone from speaking at the same time and to ensure knowing *who* is speaking. Check the learners know these rules in their own language – to be able to apply them in English.

What language do they need? This depends on level and personal needs. Find out:

- What calls do your learners make – asking for information, exchanging information, arranging meetings? The language related to these situations can then be taught.
- What do they find difficult? Some find it easy to discuss business but difficult to make small talk before getting down to business. Others find listening a problem, especially to speakers with a variety of accents, or with native speakers. Work on developing their general listening skills.
- For any level, it is important to learn and practise 'checking and clarifying' language so they can take control of conversations. Practise spelling names and taking messages.

How can they practise? Roleplays (best of all, written by the learners) are the ideal way. Make the situation realistic:

- In a one-to-one lesson, either of you can go to a different room, creating a more authentic situation.
- If teaching a group, make sure they sit back-to-back to simulate the lack of visual support.

Emailing

What are the issues? Emailing is different to most other business skills, with its focus on writing and reading. It is a key business skill but not a natural one – it has to be learnt, through instruction and practice. Writing is rarely the main reason why learners attend a language course, as it is often associated with 'school' English and can be seen as a dry and lonely activity. So make writing in your lessons as interesting as possible!

Where do learners need help? With a large variety of problems. Accuracy is one area. Although accuracy in emailing is often considered less important than in other business correspondence, it is still vital to make the learners' emails easy to understand – to avoid misunderstandings – and professional.

- Translation is one reason for lack of accuracy, often due to the use of bilingual dictionaries or online translation programs.
- Another problem is lack of knowledge of a range of fixed phrases, and poor editing skills.

Email has no set rules or conventions. Instead, it has its own 'netiquette', which recommends that emails should be polite, concise and replied to within a short time. As well as writing accurately, using conventional phrases and an appropriate formal or informal tone, learners need to write fluently and respond quickly. Emails need to be clearly structured so the reader can quickly understand the message and respond appropriately.

How can I teach emailing realistically? Use word processing whenever possible – and ensure the learners know how to use the spell checker! Business professionals can provide you with authentic emails as your main resource – so long as they are happy for you to share these with other members of the group.

- Learner emails give you typical scenarios and contexts. Use names and subject lines from their own emails to make your materials even more relevant.
- When they practise writing, make sure they use their own name and facts related to their own job.

What do I need to know? Find out exactly what kind of emails your business professionals write and receive before your emailing lessons. Do a Question and Answer session or prepare a questionnaire:

- Who they are writing to – since this determines the style of the email: writing to colleagues who they know well is much less formal.
- Why they are writing – asking for information, complaining, apologising? This determines the type of functional language to teach.

Presentations

What types of presentations do learners give? When talking about presentations, learners mean different things. Presentations in business are usually extended, pre-prepared talks where a speaker gives an audience information. This can be very formal – at an Annual General Meeting (AGM) – or informal – in a departmental meeting. A presentation usually includes some visual support – on a flipchart or with PowerPoint – and can last between a few minutes and over an hour.

Do I teach how to present? English teachers are not skills trainers and your job is to deal with *language*, not how to use software to write slides – so teach useful phrases, help to improve intonation and to make slides accurate. However, there are sometimes 'grey areas' – when giving feedback on a presentation, it is sometimes important to include non-linguistic factors such as body language or use of visuals.

What problems do learners have? Learners often mention they are much more nervous when giving a presentation in English – they will look less professional if they make mistakes or forget what to say. Give them lots of practice to improve their confidence.

- **Vocabulary** Some learners may search for vocabulary while speaking and therefore have a lot of hesitation, while others use inaccurate vocabulary. Higher-level learners may even use complicated vocabulary – idiomatic language – that other non-native speakers of English (often their audience!) may not understand.
- **Delivery** Some learners sound monotonous, others are strongly influenced by their L1. Some use their slides as a crutch – including too much text, which they then read while giving the presentation.
- **Signposting** 'Signal' phrases inform the audience where the presenter is up to – especially important if the audience includes non-native speakers, who might be following with difficulty. Signposting phrases are the frame into which presenters can put the content – learning these fixed expressions helps

them to feel less nervous when presenting in English.
- **Visuals** Any mistakes made while speaking will be gone the next minute. Any mistakes on visuals will be projected on a screen for all to see and may be extremely distracting for the audience. Visuals must be accurate. Remember that many learners – secretaries or assistants – may never *give* presentations in English, but may have to *prepare* them, including the visuals.

Many learners say that they sound less convincing when presenting in English and therefore cannot win over their audience, or that they have difficulties fielding questions that come up.

Where do I start? The learners probably know more than you do – so start with them! What do they need? What do they already know? They have possibly given many presentations in English and are aware of their weaknesses.

- Talk about their experiences and draw on them.
- Talk about training courses they have attended and good/bad presentations they have listened to.

Remind them they can transfer to English the knowledge they already have in their own language.

So what should I focus on? At the beginning of a series of lessons on presentations, come up with criteria that you and the learners can use for assessment. Focus mostly on *language* aims:

- To build vocabulary related to the presentation
- To learn and practise signposting language
- To work on intonation and pronunciation
- To practise preparing and presenting visuals
- To practise presenting to international audiences

What if they just want me to listen and give feedback? Set up clear objectives for the lesson: Ask what you should specifically listen for, write down a list of criteria and use these to help you structure the feedback you give at the end of the presentation.

What can the others do when one person is presenting? Set up listening tasks – the 'audience' can think of a question to ask at the end. Or they can focus on giving feedback on one aspect of a presentation – the effective use of signposting language, for example.

What feedback should I concentrate on? Get the learners to write a list of 'Dos and Don'ts' which can be used as criteria on which to base your comments. A feedback form helps you to structure your notes while the learners are giving their presentation – include everything from opinions on the presentation itself to grammar, vocabulary and pronunciation problems.

The language of business

Meetings and discussions

What kinds of meetings do learners attend? There are many varieties, from an informal chat with no agenda or minutes to an AGM with a very strict protocol. In between, there is a whole range – departmental, problem-solving, information-sharing, sales, kick-off, board meetings. Telephone and video conferences are also meetings. Practise the ones you think are most relevant to your learners.

What do I need to know? The first thing is to find out: What meetings in English do your learners attend? What are they about, how many people attend? Are there native or non-native speakers? How formal or informal are they? Internal, or involving people from other companies? How well do they know the other participants? This information will help you to put together activities that are relevant, and to decide if you need to focus on issues such as diplomatic language or strategies for coping with native speakers.

Find out your learners' roles in these meetings. Chairing, taking the minutes, giving opinions, or simply listening to get information? Use this knowledge to determine what language and skills to focus on.

Where do they need help? Again, it is *your* job to find out.
- Do they lack confidence speaking English in a group, especially with native speakers or colleagues higher up in company hierarchy?
- Do they find it difficult to understand exactly what people are saying – so not adding their opinions in case they have misunderstood?
- Do they find it difficult to make people understand them because they lack key vocabulary or do not have clear pronunciation?
- Do they have difficulties dealing with dominant speakers, native speakers or lower-level speakers?
- If they chair meetings, do they know the necessary phrases for summing up, moving things along, inviting people to speak or dealing with interruptions?
- If they take minutes, do they have problems understanding the details of what is said or do they have difficulties writing them up in English?

So what should I focus on? When you know what the learners do, ask probing questions to focus on the language of their meetings and prioritise in order of relevance and importance:
- Learn and practise phrases for taking part in meetings.
- Learn and practise phrases for chairing meetings.
- Extend the range of key meetings vocabulary.
- Extend the range of specialist vocabulary for taking part.
- Develop strategies for dealing with dominant speakers/native speakers/lower-level speakers.
- Practise taking and writing up minutes.

How can I give feedback? As learners take part in roleplays, complete a feedback form so you don't interrupt the activity.
- Include positive feedback as well as areas for improvement – remember to write down functional phrases that learners *do* use, and phrases that they *could* use to improve their performance.
- Write down communication difficulties that arise – like with a dominant speaker – and give strategies for how learners can deal with these.

An alternative approach is to ask your learners what *they* want feedback on and focus your attention on those areas.

Negotiating

What type of negotiations do learners take part in? This obviously depends on a business professional's job and department.
- In Human Resources, they might negotiate with future employees about salaries and contracts or with labour unions about working conditions.
- In Sales or Purchasing, they may focus on agreeing terms such as price, units and delivery times.

Ask business professionals what negotiations they take part in and make the lessons as relevant to their needs as possible. Pre-experience learners benefit from practising any negotiations that they might be confronted with in their later professional life.

Where do I start? If you have never taken part in a negotiation, spend time researching. There is plenty of information on the internet and your learners are an excellent resource. Make yourself familiar with the phases of a negotiation – Preparation, Discussion, Proposing, Bargaining, Settlement. (These stages are taken from *Negotiations* by Anne Laws, Summertown Publishing 2001.)

Preparation Go through work documents such as contracts and focus on important vocabulary. Review phrases for negotiations and practise them. Pre-experience learners might appreciate it if you give them some tips on *how* to prepare, as they probably do not have experience taking part in business negotiations.

Discussion This stage involves establishing rapport, which learners often find challenging. Equip them with

The language of business

the language for welcoming and introducing participants, and making small talk. Cultural differences will affect the amount of time spent on making small talk before a negotiation. Practise stating aims and agreeing procedures – there are functional phrases for doing this.

Proposing In this phase, negotiators put forward proposals and need to be able to ask questions politely and accurately.

Bargaining Learners need to make suggestions and respond appropriately to the proposals that have been made until a decision is reached. Teach diplomatic ways of disagreeing or making suggestions, especially if negotiating with native speakers.

Settlement This final phase involves summarising the most important points of the discussion and agreeing on any future action. The language of clarifying and checking is important, to ensure that there are no misunderstandings.

How can I help? Use these phases as a framework – skilled negotiators know how to prepare for a negotiation. What your learners need help with is preparing the *language* that they will need.

Socialising

What exactly is it? Socialising (sometimes called 'small talk') is the language connected with building relationships – functional language such as greetings and farewells, and conversation about general topics such as the weather, sports or current events. Conversations can take place over a business lunch, before a meeting starts or at the beginning of a phone call. The choice of topics will vary depending on the participants and their cultural backgrounds, but some topics – politics and religion – are rarely appropriate.

Do learners really want to practise socialising?

Business English learners usually request socialising on their course – they often feel confident about dealing with situations directly connected to their jobs, but they feel less certain when required to deal with more general topics and situations. Most business professionals are also aware that socialising is vital for successful business – it eases communication, builds rapport and creates positive relationships.

Ensure that the context is always in the business world – networking at trade fairs or introductions before a meeting starts. Find out when business professionals have to socialise, and practise the language of socialising in those contexts. With pre-experience learners, a job fair might be more appropriate.

What do they need to learn? Some learners need to learn functional phrases for greetings, introductions and farewells – *Nice to meet you, My name's ...* and *Have a safe journey home.* Such phrases are important for learners who have to make a good first impression – networking at a trade fair or business conference, or attending one-off meetings. They are especially important for lower-level learners.

- Practise strategies and language for maintaining a conversation and look at aspects of 'active' listening – asking and answering questions, learning the correct reaction (*How interesting!* or *Really?*) and when to use 'back-channelling' sounds such as *Uhuh*.
- Demonstrate the use of correct intonation patterns and increase the learners' range of vocabulary in order to be able to talk about a variety of topics.
- Analyse aspects of cultural awareness – topics which are appropriate in some cultures but not others. How important is socialising in different cultures?

How can they practise? Roleplays! These work if learners practise in contexts that they consider relevant. Check beforehand that your learners are happy playing a part different to their role in real life – and that they have the ideas, language and imagination required by the roleplay.

- Incorporate socialising into meetings/negotiation roleplays. Do some small talk for five minutes before they 'get down to business' – especially with learners who come from cultures where it isn't considered normal to small talk at the beginning of a meeting and they are dealing with cultures where it is more common.
- Build socialising sections into your lessons so that learners can practise the skills they have learned. Chatting to your learners will expose them to all the natural features of conversation outlined earlier. Ensure they practise frequently together without you being the one asking all the questions – so they have the opportunity to develop the ability to keep a conversation going themselves.
- Make the small talk more authentic by taking the learners out of the classroom to have coffee in the company canteen or the school kitchen.
- Encourage them to find opportunities to speak English outside lessons. This may include talking to a foreign colleague in the office or even joining a local English conversation group.

Telephone test

Principle Learners need to know functional phrases for taking part in routine telephone calls. Determine what phrases they already use, then follow with a feedback stage that enables them to expand their range of language before putting it to practice in a final roleplay.

Prepare
Make one set of role cards for each pair in the group and a copy of the 'Phrases framework' for every learner.

Proceed
■ Put the learners into groups of three. Give two learners (A and B) in each group the role cards. Give them a minute to read the roles and to prepare what they will say. Give Learner C the phrases framework – it is their job to write down the phrases that are used in the roleplay.

■ Make sure Learners A and B sit with their backs to their partner to simulate a phone call. Learner C makes notes of the phrases they hear.

■ When they have finished give all the learners the phrases framework. They note the phrases that they already used and think of one more additional phrase.

■ Elicit the phrases and give feedback on how they could be improved – Are they too direct or too formal? Is the pronunciation and intonation appropriate?

■ Get the learners to repeat the roleplay using all this improved language.

Higher levels To make the roleplay even more authentic, you can get the learners to write their own versions using the original role cards as a model. Give each learner two pieces of paper in the same colour – so you know which role cards go together. Ask them to think of a situation where they might speak English on the phone and write two role cards which have enough information for a roleplay. Use these when they do the roleplay for the *second* time using their improved language.

Lower levels Give more controlled practice after the feedback stage by getting the learners to write out their roleplay instead of just speaking.

One-to-one Do the roleplay with the learner and record it. This means that you won't have to make notes at the same time as you are doing the activity.

Review Keep the roleplays to use again in a review session.

Role cards

A	B
You work for ABC Technologies.	Your name is Reginald McGeever and you work for XYZ Holdings.
Your colleague, Bob Smith, is currently working on a project with XYZ Holdings, but you don't know anything about it.	You have a meeting with Bob Smith at ABC Technologies tomorrow at 11:00 but you are going to be late.
Bob is out at a meeting today and won't be back until this evening.	Call Bob to ask if you can postpone the meeting to 12:00.

Phrases framework

Introducing yourself	Asking to speak to someone
Saying someone is not available	Taking a message
Asking the speaker to repeat	Asking for the caller's name
Asking someone to spell something	Checking the message is correct
Closing the call	

No problem!

Principle Learners, if they are beginners, need to learn and use pre-fabricated phrases for their jobs, even if they do not necessarily understand all the grammar and vocabulary involved. Help them to come up with some phrases that will come in extremely useful – it is better if you know their first language well.

This idea can be adapted for whatever situation your learner might need to use English – welcoming visitors, introducing a colleague who is to give a presentation, etc.

Prepare

Be as familiar as possible with what the learners do and need. Here, they are beginners who have to answer the phone, to replace an English-speaking colleague.

Proceed

- Make a ringing noise and indicate that the learners have to answer the phone. Elicit what they would usually say, and write this on the whiteboard.

- Give a response – *Hello, can I speak to Kate Cox, please?* Elicit a reply. Feed in language, or accept suggestions in their first language and translate. Write it all up.

- Build up a dialogue like the one below, remembering to include phrases for checking and clarifying. Keep it very simple – if your learners are absolute beginners it may be better to ask the caller to ring back later!

A: Good morning. JCD.	A: Who's calling?
B: Hello, can I speak to Kate Cox, please?	B: It's Mike Holler.
A: Could you repeat that, please?	A: Just a moment, please – I'll put you through.
B: Yes, I'd like to speak to Kate Cox, please.	B: Thanks a lot.
	A: No problem.

- The learners should copy it, to keep for reference.

- Drill them saying the 'A' phrases. On the board, delete the words from the 'A' phrases, one at a time, until none are left and the learners can remember them.

- The learners practise the dialogue in pairs. Get them to underline some parts – the name, the time the person will be back – and to substitute different elements.

Follow-up Record the learners saying the phrases correctly and email them the recording – to remember how to pronounce them. This is very useful for auditory learners.

Review In the next lesson, the learners practise the substitution dialogue again. Learner A can do it without notes.

Learner autonomy Suggest they keep the phrases on cards or on a list by their phone, to refer to them as necessary.

Open the call

Principle Learners need to feel confident when starting a phone call, but frequently have difficulties with the opening moments. How much 'small talk' to make before beginning the business? Reassure them that phrases are often fixed and can be learned by heart.

Prepare

Find out how common it is in the culture of your learners to make small talk at the beginning of phone conversations. In some it is quite normal, but in others it is not.

You might find blank cards for each learner in the group useful.

Proceed

- Ask if it is normal in the learners' culture to make small talk at the beginning of a phone conversation – explain that in some cultures it is expected.

- Elicit possible small talk questions for the start of a telephone call and write these on the board/flipchart. Starting with 'How are you?', the learners may add:
  - *How's it going?*
  - *How was your weekend/holiday?*

- Point out that 'How was your …?' could follow anything the conversation partner mentioned recently – if they had a big meeting that week you could ask about it.

- Elicit a phrase to move away from this small talk section and begin the main part of the call – *'The reason I'm calling is …'*. Write this up.

- Ask the learners to think about a person they speak to regularly on the telephone. Give them two minutes to brainstorm everything they know about this person:
  - Where they are from
  - Recent holidays
  - Family
  - Hobbies
  - How long they have been with the company

- In pairs, they roleplay the opening to a conversation with this person, asking at least two small-talk questions before using the transition phrase to move onto the main business.

- Set a time limit – they have to talk for two minutes.

Follow-up To practise giving answers to the questions, ask the learners to write on cards a similar profile to the one above, but of themselves, giving only information that a person they have regular phone calls with knows about them – where they are from/recent holidays, etc. Put them into pairs to roleplay the opening of a conversation where they receive a call. Their partner asks the questions.

Politeness, please

Principle Learners need to be able to deal courteously with business partners on the telephone. Raise awareness of the features of polite language – use an exaggerated version of a 'bad' conversation to demonstrate the negative effect of language which is too direct.

Prepare
Make copies of the 'Imperfect version' and copies of the 'Improved version' opposite for every two or three learners.

Proceed

■ Give out the 'bad' version to the group. Elicit what is wrong with this conversation (it is too direct, no polite forms are used).

■ Put the learners into pairs and get them to write a better version. Each pair or small group then compares their version with another pair.

■ Give out the improved version, but stress that this is not the 'right' answer and that some of their ideas might be just as good. Monitor, to check the learners' versions and answer any questions.

■ Elicit examples of what makes language more polite:
  ● Using *could* instead of *can*, *would* instead of *will*
  ● Using indirect questions instead of direct questions: *Could you tell me when he will be back?* vs *When will he be back?*
  ● Using fixed phrases: *I'm sorry, could you repeat that please?* instead of *What?*
  ● Using *please*

■ Ask the learners for examples from their working lives where using polite phrases is very important.

Alternative Make a recording of the two versions of the conversation (ask a colleague to take the part of the other speaker) and then type up the conversation.
  ● In the first version, the intonation should be flat and sound very abrupt.
  ● The second version should have a much wider intonation range, as this is another way native speakers make their language more polite and it is useful to raise the learners' awareness of this.
The learners listen to the second version, mark arrows on their copies to indicate where the intonation rises or falls and mark the stressed word. They then read along with the recording, copying the intonation patterns.

One-to-one Do the roleplay with the learner and record it. In the next lesson, follow the same procedure as above. Then make a second recording of the conversation – the learner to listen and checks if their intonation patterns have improved.

Imperfect version

A: Hello?
B: I want to speak to Mr. Smith.
A: Who are you?
B: Bertie Black.
A: What?
B: Bertie Black.
A: Mr Smith isn't here.
B: When is he going to be back?
A: I don't know.
B: Tell him to call me back.
A: OK.
B: Bye.

Improved version

A: Hello, Anna speaking.
B: Could I speak to Mr. Smith, please?
A: Who's calling, please?
B: Bertie Black.
A: Sorry, could you repeat that please?
B: Bertie Black.
A: I'm afraid Mr Smith is out of the office at the moment, Mr Black.
B: Do you know when he might be back?
A: I'm sorry, I don't. Would you like to leave a message?
B: Yes, please would you ask him to call me back?
A: No problem, I'll make sure he gets the message. Thank you for calling. Goodbye.
B: Goodbye.

Clarify and check

Principle Learners need to have the language to check that they understood correctly – at all levels. It is especially important when they have to take down details like names or phone numbers.

Prepare

Prepare cards for each learner in the group with surnames which are difficult to spell. Get ideas from the internet or use names from your family or favourite TV programme.

Proceed

■ Explain that you are going to give the learners a card with a name on it. They are going to call their partner and leave a message for a colleague to call them back. Elicit the opening of the call and write it on the board/flipchart:

> A: *Hello, 'X' speaking.*
> B: *Hello, this is … . Can I speak to Mr Clarke, please?*
> A: *I'm sorry, he's not available at the moment. Can I take a message?*
> B: *Yes, please ask him to call me back.*
> A: *Could you spell your name for me, please?*

■ Elicit phrases the learners can use to help if they don't understand the spelling and to check what they have written is correct:

  - Can you repeat that/say that last letter again, please?
  - Sorry, I didn't catch that.
  - Was that B or P?
  - Can I read that back to you, please?
  - Let me just check I got that right.

■ The person spelling the name may also need some phrases, especially if they are unsure of the alphabet themselves:

  - *Sorry, let me start again/repeat that.*
  - *Sorry, I meant to say …*

■ Put the learners into pairs and get them to roleplay the conversation. Some pairs can do their conversations for the group. Give feedback and then get them to exchange roles: the caller becomes the receiver, and vice-versa.

Alternative Instead of thinking of names yourself, give out blank cards – the learners write down the name of a colleague or someone they know with a difficult name. They exchange the cards with another pair and make the phone call, as above. This can lead into a discussion about who these people are and how often they speak to them.

Spelling You could introduce the NATO phonetic alphabet:

  - A for Alpha …
  - B for Bravo …
  - C for Charlie …

Writing in progress

Principle Learners need to be aware of the process they go through when they write in their own language – to be able to transfer this to writing in English, especially more complex emails. Provide a guide to good practice which can be re-used in future activities. This is a good lead-in to a series of email lessons or a writing workshop.

Prepare

Make a set of the following cards for every two learners:

Collect information.	Think about who you are writing to.	Think about why you are writing.
Decide what to write.	Organise the information.	Start writing.
Finish the first draft.	Read and edit.	Write another draft.
Read again.	Edit again.	Send.

Proceed

■ Ask the learners to think about what they do when they write emails in their own language:

  - Do they make notes?
  - Do they think for a while first?
  - Do they just start writing?

■ Put them into pairs to compare what they usually do.

■ Give each pair a set of cards and get them to put the cards in one possible order for writing emails. Monitor, and check the order is sensible. Get the pairs to compare with other pairs.

■ The learners then discuss whether they follow this procedure when writing emails in English. Might it help them to write better emails?

Alternative Encourage the learners to draw a mindmap or make notes of ideas to include in their email. Before writing, encourage them to organise the content into 'beginning, middle and end', making sure they use linking and organising phrases – *firstly*, *next*, *in conclusion*, etc.

Test-Teach-Test Get the learners to write an email before you follow up with the card-matching activity, then to write a second email following your stages. They then compare the two emails. This works especially well if the learners have access to word processors in class, and can edit.

Review Re-use the cards before future writing activities, to remind the learners of good practice. They can be useful to teach writing other documents, like reports.

The right structure

Principle Learners need to be able to write clear and easy-to-read emails. This increases the likelihood that the reader will respond quickly – either answering the email or doing what the writer wants them to do. Teach them standard structures and strategies.

Prepare

Make copies of the two emails opposite for each learner in the group. One email uses a clear structure and the other does not. Also prepare a handout (one per learner) with an email structure for the learners to refer to, similar to the example opposite.

Proceed

- Give out both your emails and tell the learners to decide which one gets the message across more clearly, and why.

- Put them into pairs to look at the second email more closely and decide what structure it follows. As feedback, show them the structure you have prepared.

- Get the learners to write replies to the email with their partner, following the structure.

- The learners then exchange their emails with another pair to compare and check if they have followed the structure.

Follow-up Tell the learners to imagine the following situation: they have just come back from two days' holiday and have to respond to all the emails in their in-box. Give out six to eight emails, some of which are well structured and some which are not. Firstly get the learners to decide:

- Which emails would they respond to immediately?
- Which ones would wait?
- Which get their message across more clearly?

Get them to notice the structure and write replies.

Lower levels Use the following structure to help the learners understand emails that they receive – they focus on the main points, instead of trying to understand every word. The learners fill in the framework as they read their emails:

	Email 1	Email 2	Email 3
Purpose			
Details			
Action			

Business professionals Suggest they write their own example emails, using a situation from their working lives.

Review Get the learners to write an email on a similar topic and then follow the steps of the procedure above. Get them to go back to their original email and make changes to the structure so that it is clearer and easier to read.

Email 1

Subject: Meeting

Dear Bob,

I was talking to Janet Jones yesterday and she mentioned that the date of the team meeting hasn't been finalised yet. She mentioned that the meeting might be during the last week of April. I just wanted to bring to your attention that I am on holiday until the end of April. If at all possible, it would be great if we could have the meeting at the start of May because I really would like to attend.

I'm sorry if this causes any problems but I just wanted to get in touch before you set the date.

Kind regards,

Lucy

Email 2

Subject: Date of next team meeting

Dear Bob,

I'm writing about the date of the next team meeting and to ask if it could take place in the first week of May.

The reason for this is that I am on holiday until the end of April. I really would like to attend the meeting and therefore I would appreciate it if it could take place when I am back in the office in May.

I'm sorry if this causes any problems and I look forward to receiving details of the meeting when they are finalised.

Kind regards,

Lucy

Email structure

Subject line:	Order confirmation
Salutation:	*Dear Mr Smith, Dear Bob, Hi Janet*
Purpose:	Introduction – giving the reason for writing
Details:	Main body – giving further details
Action:	Final sentence – stating what future action is expected
Closure:	*Kind regards,*

The right phrase

Principle Learners need to know standard functional language they can use in emails. They need phrases for the following:

- An introductory paragraph – giving the reason for writing
- The main body of the email – giving further details
- A final sentence – stating what future action is expected

This is a good follow-up to *The right structure* on page 57.

Prepare

Prepare some scenarios for the learners – such as organising a meeting with a supplier – and make one set for every two learners.

Cut up phrases like the ones opposite into strips.

Proceed

■ Give the learners the scenarios and get them to write the email. Remind them to use the structure from the activity *The right structure* – purpose, details, action.

■ Now give out the phrases on slips and get the learners to sort them into structure categories. In groups, they then brainstorm more phrases for each category.

■ Get them to rewrite their emails using the phrases. They compare their original version with the new version and note the differences.

■ Depending on your teaching situation you could make copies of their emails and pass them out to the whole group, or ask the learners to write them on OHTs. In this way the whole group can participate in the discussion.

Follow-up Extend this activity by working on 'subject lines'. Point out that subject lines are also often standard, which helps the reader to understand quickly what the email is about and how important it is. Demonstrate by preparing subject lines that are concise and contain all the information needed – and some that do not. For example:

- *Agenda for meeting 24th February*
- *Meeting*
- *Confirmation of order placed 18th March*
- *Confirmation*

Get the learners to decide which subject lines are good and which not, and to refer back to the emails they have just written for comparison.

Business professionals Instead of using scenarios as prompts, ask them to bring their own emails. They rewrite them in the lesson, using the phrases. In addition, they go through them and highlight any standard phrases that are not already on the list.

I'm writing about
I'm writing to confirm/to ask/to give/to enquire
Regarding
RE:
I received your address from … and would like …
Attached is/are
Here is/are
What I specifically need is
My proposal is
My main questions are
Basically, the current situation is
Please give me your ideas on this by Friday.
Please write back by the end of the week and let me know what you think.
Please call me on my direct line/mobile on Tuesday to discuss these points.
I need this information by Wednesday. Therefore, I would appreciate it if you could get back to me by then.

The right style

Principle Learners need to be aware of formal and informal phrases and what effect these can produce. Demonstrate how even correct use of fixed phrases can sometimes seem wrong if these are too formal in an informal email, or vice-versa, or if the style is inconsistent.

Prepare

Cut up the two emails opposite into strips and put them in an envelope. Prepare enough envelopes for every two learners. Also make a complete copy of both emails for each learner.

Proceed

- Put the learners into pairs. Give each pair an envelope and get them to reassemble the two emails.

- Give each learner the complete copy to check if they have the slips in the correct order.

- Ask them to compare the style of key phrases and decide if the emails are formal or informal.

- Once basic points such as the salutation (*Dear Mr Smith* vs *Hi Anna*) have been established, get the learners to look at individual phrases in more detail. They underline any words or phrases which show that the email is formal or informal, and analyse what makes the language so. For example: using multi-word verbs (*let you know*) instead of one-word alternatives (*inform*).

- Get the learners to rewrite the emails with their partner:
  - They make the formal email more informal.
  - They make the informal email more formal.

- The pairs then compare what they have written with another pair.

- Finish by getting the learners to decide which phrases they would use for people they regularly correspond with, thinking about how well they know this person and how formal they should be.

Alternative You may wish to include, as well as functional phrases, common abbreviations used in emails and discuss when these are appropriate or not. Some of the most common business abbreviations are used in emails – for example, *asap* – but they are now combined with aspects of text messaging, eg ☺ (^_^) gr8.

Business professionals Rewrite the emails so that they relate more to your learners' jobs. It can also be helpful to look at examples of emails they bring in, particularly those from native speakers, and to search for examples of language which is very formal or informal.

Email 1

Dear Mr Smith,

I am writing regarding the sales department team event next week. I very much look forward to meeting you and the rest of the team there.

To answer your questions about my presentation:
- I will talk for around 20 minutes about 'maximising customer contact', followed by a section for questions.
- I will bring my own laptop with me but would appreciate it if you could ensure that there is a data projector in the room.

Please would you also inform me of how many people are expected to attend, once your arrangements are finalised. As I will be preparing the presentation at the end of the week, I would appreciate it if you could send me the information by Wednesday.

I am grateful for the opportunity to work with you and your team and I hope this is the beginning of a successful partnership.

Yours,

Anna Brown.

Email 2

Hi Anna,

Thanks for the info about the team event.

Presentation sounds gd, but do you think 20 mins is enough? Last year it went on for about 45 mins. Can you ask Margaret what she thinks?

No probs re the projector. I'll sort it out.

At the mo we have about 20 people registered but there'll probably be more by the end of the week. I'll let you know.

Cheers,

Chris

Preposition search

Principle Learners need to revisit standard phrases for correspondence regularly so that they start to use them actively. Do this activity in a review lesson or as a follow-up to a lesson on correspondence.

Prepare
Prepare an email. It can be one you make up, related to the learners' jobs, or one that your learners have provided which they have received. Rewrite it, taking out the prepositions. Also write in bold the words that the learners need to look up in the dictionary to find the missing preposition:

> We are writing _____ **reference** _____ your email _____
> 12 October. We are **sorry** _____ the problems that you had.
>
> Unfortunately, we **sent** your goods _____ the wrong customer
> _____ **mistake**.
>
> We **apologise** _____ any inconvenience this has caused.
>
> We **look forward** _____ doing **business** _____ you in the
> future.

Make one copy of the email for each learner in the group and provide one monolingual dictionary for every two or three learners.

Proceed
- Put the learners into groups of two or three. Give each group one copy of the email.

- Ask them to fill in the gaps with the correct preposition. See how many they can do on their own without any help.

- Give each learner a copy of the email, then direct them to the first word in bold. Get them look up the word in the dictionary to check if they have the correct preposition and then continue the procedure for each word.

- Monitor to check that they have the correct answer.

Follow-up Ask the learners how monolingual dictionaries can help them with written correspondence. As homework, ask them to make a list of all the advantages they can think of, to discuss next lesson. For example: *When writing emails, to check if I have the correct preposition.*

Higher levels Make the activity more challenging by just taking out the prepositions and not leaving any blanks. Alternatively, you can take out the verbs and get them to remember them, based on the prepositions.

Fluent and quick

Principle Learners need to develop the skill to produce an email under pressure – they often complain it takes them too much time to write in English, perhaps because they do not follow a structure, use appropriate phrases or reduce their text especially in replies when the original information is attached. Help them to work more efficiently.

Prepare
Create email writing tasks such as the one below. You will need three or four tasks, each with a different subject line.

> *You have three minutes to write the following email:*
> To:
> From:
> Subject: Request for information

Proceed
- Give the learners the writing tasks. Tell them that they have three minutes to write each one.

- Stop them after the three minutes and tell them to move on to the next one. Continue until they have done each task.

- Ask them to go back through their emails and check if they are easy to read – that they organised the content in a way that enables the reader to know quickly how to respond. They should also focus on fixed phrases, linking words and consistent formal or informal language.

- They pass on their emails to another person, who has to respond in two minutes.

- Look at the responses together: Can they shorten them? When do they need to write a *full* response? When not? Possible answers:
  - One line or one word – such as 'OK' – is enough when the original mail contains all the information.
  - The salutation may be left out if it is very informal or when the email is part of a longer exchange.
  - The closure may be left out if it is very informal – email addresses always say who the message is from.

Alternative Instead of getting the learners to respond to the emails, get them to cut the number of words. This will help them to write more fluently. First explain the task: they each receive an email to summarise.
- The first person reduces from 50 to 40 words.
- The second person from 40 to 30 words.
- The third person from 30 to 20 words.
- Finally, the first person to fewer than 10 words!

Set a time limit for each edit, then put the learners together to compare the last message with the original and to discuss how much of the meaning is lost.

Correspondence vocabulary

Principle Learners need to understand vocabulary used in standard email phrases which is above their current language level. Build dictionary skills into the lesson and show them a useful tool that they can use in the office when they are writing.

Prepare

Make copies of the 'Vocabulary for correspondence' handout opposite for each learner in the group and provide a monolingual dictionary for every two or three learners.

Proceed

■ Put the learners into groups of two or three. Give each group a monolingual dictionary and each learner a copy of the handout. Ask them to complete Part A in their groups, using their monolingual dictionary to check that they have the correct definitions.

■ Then get them to look up the word 'complain'. Direct their attention to the sample sentences in the definition and elicit the prepositions that go with 'complain'. Elicit the differences between 'complain to' and 'complain about'.

■ Tell them that monolingual dictionaries are extremely useful for finding out the correct preposition when writing emails or letters.

■ Elicit the nouns of the verbs in Part A and write them on the worksheet. Encourage the learners to use their dictionaries to check that they have the correct noun.

■ Get the learners to look up the word 'reference' and direct them to the phrase 'with reference to'.

■ Ask the learners to use their monolingual dictionaries to complete Part B of the handout. Monitor and help as necessary.

Learner autonomy Ask the learners how monolingual dictionaries can help them with written correspondence. For example: *Use dictionaries when writing emails, to check if I have the correct preposition.*

See Chapter 1 for more ideas on using monolingual dictionaries in lessons.

Correspondence vocabulary

Part A

Write a definition for each verb.

To refer	
To enquire	
To request	
To complain	
To apologise	
To confirm	
To attach	
To enclose	

Part B

With reference _____ your email _____ 12 December.

I am writing to complain _____ the late delivery.

I am writing to apologise _____ the damaged goods.

I am writing to request information _____ your new range of products.

I am writing inquire _____ the presentation seminar that you are offering in January.

Linking it up

Principle Learners need to make their emails easy to follow by using linking words and expressions. Give them a comprehensive example of a sequenced text to practise identifying the linking words and their function.

Prepare
Make copies of the worksheet for each learner in the group.

Proceed
- Explain the scenario.
- Give out the worksheet. Set a comprehension task and ask the learners to read it.
- Get them to read it again, underlining any linking words or expressions in the email. Then get the learners to categorise the highlighted words under the following headings:

Sequencing	Result	Addition	Contrast

- Monitor, and then check and discuss.
- Elicit additional linking words the learners might know *already* and add them to the appropriate category.
- Add any more useful linking expressions that you think they *should* know.

Lower levels Write a simpler version of the scenario and focus on fewer linking words and phrases.

Business professionals Get them to write about a similar problem, related to their own jobs.

Key (Some other possibilities are added in *italics*.)

Sequencing		Result	
Firstly	*In addition*	Therefore	*As a*
Secondly	*Next*	So	*consequence*
Finally	*After that*	Consequently	*Thus*
In summary	*Lastly*	As a result	
		Due to this	

Addition		Contrast	
And	*In addition*	But	*Nevertheless*
Furthermore	*Too*	However	*Although*
Moreover			*Even though*
			Yet
			Despite this

Scenario

There was a huge problem recently in your company. Monthly bills are usually printed and arrive with the customers around the 18th of every month.

However, in December, 1,000 customers received 'final warning' bills even though they did not owe any money to the company, and these bills were delivered to your customers in the UK on December 24th, Christmas Eve!

The CEO has found out about this and wants an explanation of exactly how it happened. The matter is investigated, and an email written to the CEO.

Worksheet

Dear Ms Smith,

As requested, I am writing to explain what happened in December leading to the delivery of final warning bills on December 24th, many of which were incorrect.

Several factors contributed to this regrettable situation.

Firstly, we outsourced printing the bills to a printing company in order to cut costs. This was the first time we had used this company and therefore we did not know how reliable they were.

Secondly, our server crashed and so we were not able to send the later data to the printing company as planned.

Furthermore, the printing company had a problem with their printer and had to wait two days for a new part. Consequently, the bills were not printed until December 18th, which was five days later than agreed. We called the company on December 19th for an update but our contact person was off sick so we left a message. However, no one from the company contacted us.

Finally, the bills were posted on December 20th. As a result, they were delivered on December 24th. 1,000 customers received final warning bills in error. Due to this, and especially as it was Christmas Eve, they were very angry. Many people called to complain and, moreover, some want to cancel their policies with us.

In summary, this mistake was caused by several different factors. It has resulted in terrible damage to our reputation and has also lost us several good customers.

Please let me know if you have any additional questions.

Regards,

Confidence counts

Principle Learners need to build a lot of confidence when giving presentations in another language. Tell them they are better at presenting in English than they think!

Prepare

Think about a bad presentation you have been to. If you don't have much business experience, you could think about boring speeches you have heard, boring lectures you attended while studying or have seen on TV. You can also do an internet search on 'Death by PowerPoint' – for pictures of business people falling asleep during presentations.

You will need flipchart paper, an OHT or a PowerPoint slide.

Proceed

■ Use your internet pictures to elicit examples of bad presentations that your learners have experienced. Ask questions – *Have you ever felt like the person in the picture?* – to lead into your 'bad presentation' story.

■ Tell the learners about *your* experience of a bad presentation. Describe it and how you felt both during and at the end of it. Encourage questions.

■ Explain that the learners are going to tell a story about the worst business presentation they have ever been to. It could be in English or in their own language. Set a time limit for them to prepare.

■ In pairs, get them to talk about their experiences and draw conclusions from their discussions. Write these up on a flipchart, OHT or PowerPoint slide. For example:
  • Badly prepared
  • Too many visuals or not enough visuals
  • Visuals with too much detail
  • Flat intonation making the speaker sound boring
  • Too long or too fast
  • The wrong audience in mind – too technical or not technical enough
  • Bad body language
  • Spoken entirely from the paper, without looking up

■ Get the learners to reflect on which of the problems on the board *they* make when giving presentations in English. Cross out the things that they don't have problems with.

■ Point out that they already have a lot of experience to draw on – this will help them when they present in English.

Pre-experience learners Get them to talk about the worst presentation that one of their professors has given.

Review Keep the flipchart paper/OHT/PowerPoint slide. After a series of lessons on presentations, bring out the list again. Ask the learners what they can now cross off the list.

Dos and don'ts

Principle Learners need to improve both their confidence and fluency, and mini-presentations are a great tool for doing this. Help them to feel less nervous and more professional when giving a presentation in English.

Prepare

Read up on *dos* and *don'ts* for presenting. You can find information on the internet, and many business English coursebooks include 'Golden Rules'. Based on what you find, make sets of mini-presentation cards for every three or four learners in the group:

Know your audience well.	Keep slides simple.	Read from cards.
Summarise.	Mumble.	Look at one person.

You will also need flipchart paper.

Proceed

■ Put the learners into groups of three or four and give each group a set of cards. Ask them to sort them into *dos* and *don'ts* for making presentations. Elicit answers and write them up on the flipchart, to refer to later.

■ Tell each learner to choose one card and to prepare a mini-presentation about it. They should focus on why the *do* or *don't* on their card is important when presenting.

■ Get them to take turns presenting. After each presentation, encourage feedback based on the list of *dos* and *don'ts*.

Follow-up If you are beginning a series of lessons on presentations using this activity, at the end of the lesson ask: *So, which of these 'dos' and 'don'ts' can I help you with as your English teacher?* Prioritise which aspects the learners would like to focus on during the course, and use this information to plan future lessons.

Alternative Instead of using cards, elicit *dos* and *don'ts* from the learners and write them up on the flipchart. Then get each learner to choose one for their mini-presentation.

Review Bring the list of *dos* and *don'ts* to future lessons on presentations. Get the learners to refer to the list every time they give a presentation in lessons (and outside!) and to reflect on what they did well and what they could do better next time.

Build up and break down

Principle Learners need to increase their range of work-related vocabulary – especially if they have just taken on new jobs and have to give presentations on new topics. This activity works best with one-to-one learners but can also work with small groups.

Prepare

In advance of the lesson, ask your learners to give you copies of presentations they give. Go through them and note the main topics. A bilingual dictionary may be useful during the lesson.

Proceed

■ Write the main topic of the presentation on the board/flipchart and draw a circle around it. Ask what the key points are. Write these up as well:

■ Brainstorm vocabulary around each of the key points. Write the words around the circles for each one. If necessary, the learners check unknown words in the dictionary and note down if the words are nouns, verbs, etc. Practise pronunciation and mark the stress patterns.

■ Ask the learners to prepare a short presentation on the topic, using as many of the words as possible. They can refer to the words on the board/flipchart when giving the presentation but they cannot refer to their notes.

■ Get them to give their presentation and you all give feedback on the accuracy and range of vocabulary.

■ Erase half of the words. Get them to give the presentation again. After the presentation, give further feedback.

■ Erase *all* the words and get the learners to give the presentation one more time. Again, give feedback.

Higher levels Focus on extending the range of vocabulary that the learners already have. The learners give their presentations first, and you write down key words you hear. Write these words up on the board/flipchart and brainstorm other words that express the same meaning.

Pronunciation If you notice the learners have difficulty pronouncing key words, drill them and show them online dictionaries that have pronunciation functions.

Review In the next lesson, check what the learners remember – choose some of the words and get them to use them to give the presentation again.

Learner autonomy They add the words to their card box.

Choose your criteria

Principle Learners need to be aware of specific areas where they can improve their presenting skills. Help them to become more familiar with their own strengths and weaknesses by giving each other specific feedback.

Prepare

Ask the learners to bring to the next lesson three or four slides of a presentation that they give in their jobs.

Proceed

■ Tell the learners that they will be giving each other feedback on their presentation skills. Elicit possible criteria and write them up on the board/flipchart:
  - Content
  - Signposting language
  - Fluency
  - Delivery
  - Speed
  - Grammar errors
  - Signs of nervousness
  - Range of vocabulary

■ Get them to decide which *two* areas they would like to have feedback on.

■ They give their presentations and then receive feedback based on the chosen criteria.

■ Afterwards, get the learners to do their presentations again, focusing on one aspect where they need to improve.

Alternative Film the presentations. Get the learners to compare their first version with their second version – to note where they made improvement/still need to improve.

Review Ask the learners to do the same presentation again in a subsequent lesson, to reflect on areas where they made improvement and choose new areas for further practice.

Follow the signs!

Principle Learners need to know and use signposting phrases, for their presentations to be well-organised and easy to follow. Teach these phrases so that they can use them as a framework into which they put their content.

Prepare
Make a copy of the worksheet opposite for every learner and one set of cards for every two learners.

Proceed
- Put the learners into pairs and give each pair the worksheet and the cards. Ask them to decide which section each phrase belongs to. They compare, then check with you.

- Once all the cards are placed in the correct sections, get the learners to write the phrases onto their copy of the worksheet. Check the pronunciation, and practise if necessary.

- Ask the learners to prepare a mini-presentation on a topic of their choice. It should only last a few minutes, but should contain as many of the signposting phrases as possible.

- They give their presentations to the group. As the others listen, they pick up cards with any phrases they hear. At the end, check how many phrases were used by counting the cards.

Lower levels Limit the language you teach, with only one or two phrases in each section.

Higher levels Start by putting the learners into pairs, give out the worksheet and get them to brainstorm phrases they already know for each section. (In one-to-one classes, get the learner to tell *you*.) Check their answers carefully, as learners sometimes pick up phrases from colleagues which are incorrect. Give out the cards, and do the activity as above.

Review Type out the phrases, with one word blanked out – *I've _____ my talk into three parts* (divided) – and get the learners to fill them in, or give out the worksheet again in a future lesson and see how many phrases the learners can remember, before comparing with the worksheet they filled in previously.

Signposting worksheet

Introducing the presentation and giving an overview	Starting the main presentation
Concluding each point	Moving on to the next point
Referring to other points	Summarising and concluding

Signposting phrases

Today, I'm going to talk about …	I'm going to tell you about …	I've divided my talk into three parts …
Firstly … secondly … finally …	The presentation should take around 30 minutes.	I'd like to begin by …
The first thing I'd like to talk about is …	Starting with …	I'll begin by …
So, I've told you about …	We've looked at …	That's all I'm going to say about …
Now I'd like to look at …	Let's move on to …	Turning to …
As I mentioned earlier …	We'll be looking at this in more detail later on.	… as we saw in the first part of my talk.
Let's quickly summarise what we've looked at.	So, in conclusion, I have told you about …	Finally, let me recap the issues we've covered.

Stand and deliver!

Principle Learners need to be able to 'speak' their presentations effectively, which can be challenging. Make them aware of their intonation patterns and help them to improve how they communicate with their audience.

Prepare

Make a recording of yourself giving the introduction to a presentation. Record it in three different versions:

- Version A: normal speed, with pauses
- Version B: too fast
- Version C: flat intonation, with hesitation

Prepare a transcript as a handout for every learner in the group. Also prepare a PowerPoint slide/OHT of the transcript with the stressed words underlined (as in Version A) – putting a slash between the words where there is a break:

Good morning, ladies and <u>gentlemen</u> / My name is Dieter <u>Pohlmann</u> / and I am responsible for Production <u>Planning</u> /

Proceed

- Get the learners to write an introduction to a presentation and to practise it in small groups. Make a recording of each introduction and say you will refer to it later in the lesson.

- Tell them that they are going to listen to three versions of a presentation introduction and decide if the speaker is:
  - *effective*
  - *too fast*
  - *boring and flat*

- Play the recordings and elicit the differences between the three versions. Elicit what is good about Version A.

- Give out the transcript. Play Version A again. Get half the learners to underline the words that are stressed and the other half to insert slashes for the pauses. Show the PowerPoint slide/OHT and get the learners to check their answers. Elicit English intonation patterns – we tend to pause after stressed words.

- Play the recorded versions of the learners' introductions and get them to decide how they could be improved.
  - Did they speak at a suitable speed?
  - Did they stress key words?
  - Did they use intonation and pauses to give effect?

- Get the learners to practise and record their introductions again. Finally, they listen to their second recording and notice the improvements.

Learner autonomy Get the learners to assess their progress on their own. They can do this by making recordings of their presentations, and then use the three questions above to check their speed and intonation patterns.

Weatherman vs Spiderman

Principle Learners need to break the habit of reading from slides. Teach them to speak without looking at their visuals and to realise that they do not need to use their slides for support, even in English.

Prepare

Look in the internet for pictures of Spiderman and of a weatherman. Put the pictures on PowerPoint slides or OHTs.

Ask the learners to bring to the lesson slides that they present for their jobs. If you do not have access to a computer and data projector, ask them to put the slides on OHTs.

Proceed

- Show the weatherman picture and elicit how he (or she!) presents – how he rarely turns round to look at his slides.

- Show a picture of Spiderman and elicit from the learners why some business people present more like Spiderman than like the weatherman:
  - They sometimes get so nervous when presenting in English.
  - They turn their back on their audience in order to read their slides.

  This creates the impression of Spiderman crawling up the wall!

- Elicit what they can do to present like the weatherman:
  - Create slides with little text
  - Rehearse a presentation several times beforehand
  - Be very familiar with the information presented

- Get the learners to present the slides that they brought with them to the lesson.

- Give feedback. Get them to practise until they feel confident facing their audience – and not their slides.

Review Steve Jobs, founder of Apple, is well-known for being an outstanding presenter. Getting learners to present like him, you can help them to break the habit of reading from their slides. While most speakers fill their slides with text, charts and graphs, Steve Jobs does the opposite. There is very little text on his slides – most of them simply show one image or one number.

Search the internet with the key words 'macworld + keynote + steve + jobs', and choose a five-minute segment from one of his presentations to show to your learners. Get them to practise presenting slides in a Steve Jobs way and give each learner a number between 1 and 10 (1 = not at all like him, 10 = very much like him).

Learner autonomy When giving presentations, get them always to evaluate themselves on a sliding scale – How much were they the weatherman or Spiderman?

Friendly persuasion

Principle Learners need to be persuasive when giving presentations. Give them practice in making convincing arguments and in selling their ideas to their business partners.

Proceed

- Elicit what information is important when deciding to invest in a company. Write the ideas up on the board/flipchart.

- Put the learners into groups. Get each group to choose a company and prepare a presentation about it – as if they were going to present it to potential investors. If they have access to computers, they can research information about the company that they chose. If not, encourage them to invent the details.

- Set a time limit.

- Choose one person from each group to present. Tell the others that they are business investors and have €2m to invest.

- After each group has presented, the investors have a small meeting to decide how to invest the money.

Pre-experience learners Get them to prepare their presentations as if they are presenting at a 'careers fair'. Ask them to focus on the information that business students applying for jobs would find most interesting.

In-company learners If they are in different departments, get them to prepare a presentation about why their management should invest in their department or in a specific project.

Homework Give the learners the task of making PowerPoint slides based on their presentations. Use these slides as a basis for activities such as *Follow the signs!* or *Weatherman vs Spiderman* (pages 65 and 66).

Follow-up Get the learners to watch extracts from TV shows such as 'Dragon's Den' (you can see clips on YouTube) and discuss with them if they would invest in the business plans.

International delivery

Principle Learners need strategies for presenting to international audiences so that 'non-expert' and non-native speakers with a variety of language backgrounds and levels can easily understand their presentations. Raise their awareness of such strategies.

Prepare

Have ready some topics for mini-presentations, if you are going to use them in the second part of the activity.

Proceed

- Give the learners the following scenario – they have to give the same presentation to two different groups.
  - Group A consists only of native English speakers.
  - Group B consists of people from different countries, with different language backgrounds and levels.

- Put them into groups and ask them to discuss how presenting to Group A is different to presenting to Group B – with Group B, they cannot be sure that all the participants will have a high level of English.

- They make a list of tips for business people who present to international audiences, and discuss – trying to agree on the most useful:
  - Use short, simple sentences.
  - Avoid or explain colloquial, idiomatic, technical or other unfamiliar terms.
  - Repeat each important idea, using different words to explain the same concept.
  - Use appropriate facial and hand gestures to emphasise the meanings of words.
  - Pause more frequently.
  - Don't assume that the audience understands – in fact, assume that they don't.

- Give each group a topic for a mini-presentation, or get them to choose their own. Tell them to prepare it for a very heterogeneous Group B. Set a time limit.

- They give their presentations. The others listen and give feedback, based on the strategies they came up with for presenting to an international audience.

Follow-up Get the learners to go through their own presentations and note words that a lower-level learner/non-expert might not understand. In the next lesson, they give their presentations – *without* using these words.

Review When the learners are doing speaking activities, note down language they use that a lower-level learner or a non-expert might not understand. Write this up on the board and elicit how they could explain the words so that non-native speakers *can* understand them.

It's simply (present) perfect!

Principle Learners need to be able to present information using PowerPoint effectively. Review at the same time both a grammatical structure and the language of presentations.

Prepare

You will need to have access to computers and PowerPoint. Make a PowerPoint slide with *Dos* and *Don'ts* for effective visuals. Include instructions such as those opposite.

Also make PowerPoint slides about grammatical structures that you have covered during the course and fill them with as much information as possible. Save these and bring to the lesson or, if possible, email them to your learners to save onto their laptops. See opposite for an example for the present perfect.

Proceed

- Put learners into groups and get them to brainstorm *Dos* and *Don'ts* for effective slides. Elicit ideas and then get them to compare their lists to yours.

- Assign each group a grammatical structure and tell them to brainstorm what they remember about it.

- Refer them to your PowerPoint slide about the structure. Get them to say if it is effective or not, and why. Then get the learners to compare what they remember with what is on the slide. Clarify any questions they might have.

- Tell the learners that they are going to prepare a presentation about the structure. They use your slide and their ideas to create *three* effective slides of their own about the structure.

- Get the learners to practise explaining the grammatical structure in their small group. Remind them to use signposting language, etc.

- Assign one learner from each small group to present to the whole group. You all give feedback.

Review Tell the learners to bring in slides that they present for their jobs. Get them to show their slides to the group and give each other feedback. Give them time to make changes to the slides before getting them to actually present them to the group.

Learner autonomy Using the internet, they look at presentations from well-known business people such as Bill Gates and analyse the slides.

A good source for this is:
www.ted.com
Another good source is the site from Garr Reynolds:
www.garrreynolds.com

Effective slides

- Don't write full sentences, just key words.
- Don't include much more than one point on each slide.
- Don't use more than one or two slides per minute of your presentation.
- Don't use too much colour, animation or sound, as this is distracting.
- Use a standard, easy-to-read font in a large size (at least 18 point).
- Use graphs and charts where possible. Make sure they are simple to understand.
- Check your slides for spelling and grammar mistakes.
- Get someone else to check them, too.

Ineffective slides

The present perfect

The present perfect is formed by using 'have' with the third form of the verb, eg *I have given a presentation; I have answered the phone.*

The present perfect is used to talk about something which started in the past and has not finished, eg *I have worked for this company for three years.*

It is also used to talk about something which happened in the past but is still relevant in the present, eg *My printer has run out of paper.*

It is also used to talk about past experience when no point in time is mentioned, eg *I have been on many business trips to China.*

In conversation and informal writing, the 'have' is usually shortened to *'ve*, eg *I've read all my emails.*

It is spoken very quickly and can be quite difficult to hear, especially when listening to native speakers.

Reviewing the situation

Principle Learners need tools for evaluating their performance. Enable them to reflect – to continue making progress outside the classroom. Review what you have done and plan with your learners what to do in the next block of lessons.

Prepare
Make copies of a self-evaluation worksheet for each learner in the group:

Reflect on your presentation and tick ✓ **the sentences that you consider to be correct:**

When I made my presentation …

____ I covered all the necessary points.

____ I had a clear structure.

____ I used signposting language to organise my talk.

____ I used language accurately:
grammar
vocabulary
pronunciation

____ I spoke at a good speed.

____ I added variety to my voice.

Proceed
■ Elicit which areas of presentations you have worked on during the course – signposting, delivery, vocabulary, etc.

■ Write the following sentence on the board:
Now I can … better when presenting in English.

■ Put the learners into small groups to discuss how they would complete the sentence. Then give each group flipchart paper to prepare a mini-presentation summing up the main areas where they have made improvement.

■ After they have given their presentations, give out the self-evaluation worksheet and get the learners to complete it. Set a time limit of about five minutes, then put them into groups to discuss their answers.

■ Discuss, as a whole-group activity, and use the results of the self-evaluation to identify further areas to work on to improve their presentation skills.

Alternative Change the questions according to what you have covered in the lessons.

Review When the learners give a real presentation in their job, encourage them to do this self-evaluation task as homework. Invite discussion in the following lesson – it will help you identify areas they are making progress in, as well as areas which still need to be developed.

What's your problem?

Principle Learners need to be aware of areas where they need to develop. Provide them with criteria for assessing performance after a meetings roleplay. This learner-centred fluency activity practises the vocabulary of meetings and works especially well as a lead-in for a workshop or series of lessons on meetings.

Prepare
Provide flipchart paper and markers for every three or four learners in the group.

Proceed
■ Put the learners into pairs or small groups and get them to write 'Difficulties in meetings' in the middle of flipchart paper and then form a mindmap around it, working together and adding things they find difficult in meetings in English. The final version might look something like this:

It takes me too long to think of what to say.

I can't understand everything.

Difficulties in meetings

My language is too direct.

I don't have enough vocabulary.

■ The groups compare their mindmaps and discuss them.

■ At the end of the discussion, ask:
  ● *Which items on the mindmaps can I help you with as your English teacher?*
  ● *Which aspects of meetings would you like us to focus on during the course?*

Review Get the learners to do more meetings roleplays and to use the mindmaps to reflect on areas where they have improved – or not!

An agenda

Principle Learners need to practise taking an active part in meetings in English. Enable them to try out new language in the safe environment of your lessons.

Prepare

Make copies of an agenda for each learner in the group. Either use the one below or use it as a framework – in other words, without these items for discussion, writing your own with what you know your learners might need to discuss.

Agenda

Welcome, introductions, apologies for absence

Minutes of the previous meeting

Items for discussion:

1 New staff canteen
The old canteen is now too small and will be replaced with a new building. We are looking for ideas on how to improve this facility.

2 Sick leave
This year has seen the highest-ever levels of people taking time off sick. We need to think of reasons why this could be happening and possible ways of dealing with it.

3 Staff party
It is nearly time for the annual staff party and we are looking for ideas on location, and other details.

Proceed

■ Hand out the agenda. Give the learners some time to read it, make notes and decide what to say.

■ Decide who is going to chair the meeting. Set a time limit which the chairperson must keep to.

■ While the meeting is taking place, listen and make notes of errors and language which can be improved, for feedback at the end.

Business professionals Instead of giving them your agenda, get them to write their own, based on their current work. You can use the 'framework' version for this.

Alternative Film the learners taking part in the meeting. Establish criteria for giving feedback. Get them to watch the recording and give each other feedback on what they did well and where they can improve, limiting their comments to the agreed criteria.

Meeting words

Principle Learners need to know vocabulary that is very specific to meetings. Show even the higher levels they may well be unaware of some essential vocabulary if they have only learned general English.

Prepare

Prepare a list of vocabulary related to meetings. Your exact list will depend on the level and needs of your learners but could include:

> *minutes, agenda, chair, item, action points, vote, move on, proposal, summarise, objective, apologies, AOB*

Provide monolingual dictionaries for every two or three learners in the group.

Proceed

■ Get the learners to make three columns on a piece of paper, each wide enough to write a word in, and add headings like this:

√	?	X

■ Explain that you are going to read out some vocabulary connected with meetings.
  - If they *know* what this word means, they should write it in the first (√) column.
  - If they *think* they know but are not *sure*, they write it in the second (**?**) column.
  - If they have *no idea*, they write it in the third (**X**) column.

■ Read out the vocabulary slowly and give the learners time to write it down. Encourage them to ask for repetition or spelling, which is also good practice.

■ In pairs or small groups, they share the information: if they have written a word in the second or third column, they ask someone who has it written in the first column for help.

■ After they have done all they can, give out the learner dictionaries or get the learners to check with an online dictionary for anything they are still not certain about. Make sure they check the pronunciation, including word stress, and practise this if necessary.

■ Finally, they write example sentences for each word they had to look up.

Follow-up Get the learners to prepare a more extended piece of writing about a recent meeting they attended.

Review They put new words in their card box. In the next lesson, they write down all the words they can remember, then check in the box which words they forgot.

My agenda

Principle Learners need vocabulary related to their specific jobs when taking part in meetings in English. Prepare them for their next meeting and also teach them strategies for the future. This activity works best with one-to-one learners but also works with small groups.

Prepare

Ask the learners to bring a meeting agenda to the lesson. Provide a monolingual dictionary or make sure you have access to an online dictionary.

Proceed

■ Ask the learners to give you background information about the meeting:
  - Who will be there?
  - Who will chair the meeting?
  - What will happen after this meeting?
  - What is your relationship with the participants?

■ Go through the agenda item by item and get the learners to brainstorm possible vocabulary which might come up:

> **Item:**
> **Marketing strategy for new sports drink**
> Possible vocabulary:
> *celebrity endorsement, billboards, sponsorship*

■ Use the monolingual dictionary to look up any vocabulary they are not sure about and check (via the example sentence) that this is exactly what they mean.

■ Get the learners to practise this vocabulary by explaining their opinion on this item and what they would like to say in the meeting.

Alternative Do this activity with an *recent* agenda. Get the learners to brainstorm vocabulary as above since it is likely to be relevant to their jobs. Then ask them to tell you what actually happened in that meeting. This is still useful as preparation for subsequent meetings or if the learners have to produce minutes or report to colleagues.

Learner autonomy Encourage them to use a similar process when they prepare for meetings in English on their own. They should go through the agenda, brainstorm vocabulary that they think they will need and use an online dictionary to check that they can pronounce the words correctly.

Be diplomatic

Principle Learners need to have an awareness of diplomatic language. Demonstrate how to say things politely and tactfully so as not to cause offence – this is especially important for those who have to deal with native speakers or very advanced non-native speakers, who are more likely to notice *how* a learner says something as well as *what* they say.

Prepare

Prepare a 'meetings' roleplay (see *An agenda* on page 70 for ideas). It needs to be one that the learners can complete in approximately ten minutes.

You will also need a digital voice recorder or a video camera.

Proceed

■ Give out the roleplay and give the learners time to prepare. Explain that you are going to record them. Set a time limit and record them while they complete the roleplay.

■ Write the following sentences on the board:
  - *I don't agree.*
  - *You should do that.*
  - *That's a bad idea.*

■ Elicit how the sentences could be more diplomatic:
  - *I'm sorry, I don't really agree.*
  - *Would it be possible for you to do that?*
  - *I'm not sure that's such a good idea.*

■ Emphasise that intonation plays an important role in diplomatic language. Read out the two versions of the sentences to the group, making sure that you use a wider range of intonation in the second version. Ask the learners what differences they notice. Practise the sentences, focusing on the intonation patterns.

■ Ask the learners to watch/listen to their roleplay and make a note of any language they used that was very diplomatic or that could be *more* so.

■ Get them to complete the roleplay again.

Alternative Some learners are resistant to using diplomatic language, preferring to be 'straight-talkers'. If that is the case, discuss the benefits of using diplomatic language in certain cultures or situations.

Follow-up See the 'Negotiations' section for more practice in diplomatic language.

Lead the meeting

Principle Learners need to be able to chair meetings efficiently, as success can depend on the skill of the chairperson. Many business professionals already have all the skills to lead meetings – give them the phrases to do it in English!

Prepare

Make a copy of the worksheet and a set of the cards for every two learners in the group. Also prepare a 'meetings' roleplay. It could be from *An agenda* on page 70, or from a photocopiable resource pack.

Proceed

■ Ask the learners to think about a recent meeting they have been to:
- Who was the chairperson?
- Did they do a good job?

■ Put them into pairs and give out the worksheet and the cards. Ask them to match the cards with the situations a chairperson needs to deal with.

■ Get them to write the phrases onto the framework, adding any other phrases that they would like to use when chairing a meeting. Monitor to check that the extra phrases are correct.

■ Set up a roleplay of a meeting and designate one learner to be the chairperson.

■ Listen and make notes on errors and language which can be improved, for later feedback. Also give the chairperson individual feedback on their performance and ask the other learners to comment.

Alternative To encourage the chairperson to use the target language, give the participants specific roles. For example:
- *Be very aggressive and keep interrupting.*
- *Be very shy and unwilling to speak.*

Higher levels Give out the worksheet *first* and get the learners, in pairs, to brainstorm phrases (or to tell you, in one-to-one classes) they already know for each section. Check their answers carefully, as they often pick up phrases from colleagues which are incorrect. Then give out the cards, and do the activity as above.

Review Type out the phrases with one word blanked out – *Let's _____ started, shall we?* – and ask the learners to fill them in. Also give them cards naming various situations in a meeting and get them to quickly come up with a phrase that they can use in each one.

Lead the meeting worksheet

Someone interrupts another speaker.	Someone is dominating the discussion.
Someone keeps going off the point.	Someone moves onto another point before the present issue is finalised.
Someone is not very clear.	Someone keeps repeating the same thing in different words.
One of the participants is very quiet.	Someone says something that is not factually correct.

Lead the meeting cards

Could you let Bob finish, please?	Please can we stick to today's agenda?
I'm sorry, could you explain that again?	Bob, do you have anything to add?
Thanks. Can we hear from some of the others, please?	Sorry, can we just finish this point before moving on?
Thanks, I think we've got that now.	Are you sure about those facts?

Take the minutes

Principle Learners need to write minutes of the meetings that they attend. Challenge them to be clear, concise, well-organised and accurate, giving them a model so that there are no misunderstandings about what was decided or who has to follow up what after the meeting.

Prepare

Make one copy of the minutes for each learner in the group.

Proceed

- Set the scene: a toy company is having a sales meeting. Get the learners to consider what might be discussed.

- Give out the minutes and ask the learners to find out if they were right.

- Put them into pairs to look at the minutes and find typical characteristics:
  - Date, location and time of meeting as well as type of meeting
  - Who attended, who chaired, who took the minutes, who could not attend
  - List of items with a brief summary of what was said
  - List of action points, who is responsible and what the deadline is
  - List of any other business
  - Date, time and location of next meeting

- Ask the learners if these characteristics are typical of *their* minutes. There will be variations in every industry, company and department, but most of these characteristics are standard.

- Set up a 'meeting' roleplay (see *An agenda* on page 70). Make sure one person is responsible for chairing it.

- After the roleplay, put the learners into pairs to write up the minutes, using the model from 'Big Toys' to help.

- Get the learners to exchange their minutes with another pair to do a peer-check, or hand them in to you for checking.

Alternative Instead of using the 'Big Toys' sales meeting, write up minutes on a topic that is related to the learners' own job or company.

Homework Get the learners to write up minutes of real meetings they attend and bring them to the next lesson. These meetings don't necessarily have to be in English, as long as they write the *minutes* in English.

There might be issues of confidentiality with real meetings, so assure the learners that you will treat all information as confidential and will not make copies. Alternatively, get them to change any sensitive information – prices or names.

Minutes
Big Toys Sales Meeting
Excel Hotel   21 April 15:00–17:30

Chairperson: Cathy Smith
Minute taker: Charlie Jones
Attendees: Pete White, Sue Parker, Jan Grey, Robert Reed
Apologies: Bob Black

Item 1
New range of soft toys
    Pete White presented the new range of soft toys for Autumn/Winter. Samples will be sent out to all sales reps by the end of this week. The R&D dept needs feedback so any necessary changes can be made in time. Final samples for showing to customers to be available from July.

Action item:
    Collect feedback from all sales reps to send to R&D.

Person responsible:
    Pete White

Deadline:
    End of May

Item 2
Sales targets YTD
    Sales reports for Q-1 are now in and are looking good. Most areas are on target, except the southern region which is slightly below. Thanks to all reps for getting the reports in on time.

Action item:
    Full sales report will be distributed to all reps.

Person responsible:
    Cathy Smith

Deadline:
    End of April

AOB
Sue Parker asked for feedback on the sales of the new Bumper Car toys so far.

Action item:
    Cathy Smith to find out this information and email to all reps by end of April.

Date of next meeting:
    26 May, Excel Hotel, 15:00

International meetings

Principle Learners need to be able to take part in meetings effectively with participants from different cultural backgrounds. Give them a context for functional phrases they can use, and then introduce the language.

Prepare

Make a copy of Worksheets A and B for each learner in the group. Also prepare a 'meetings' roleplay – from *An agenda* on page 70 or from a photocopiable resource pack.

Proceed

■ Put the learners into pairs and give out Worksheet A. Ask them to read the text, posted to a 'Young Managers' forum, and discuss three things Steve could do to manage his international meetings better.

■ Give out Worksheet B (Bob's reply) and tell the learners to read it, to see if their advice is there. They discuss with their partner if they agree/disagree with the advice.

■ As a group, write a checklist of things the learners can keep and refer to, when holding international meetings. Alongside the recommendations, the learners note useful functional phrases in each area:

- State the expected outcome of the meeting.
  By the end of this meeting, I would like to have made a decision on …
- Ask other participants for their opinions.
  Juan, what do you think about …?
- Interrupt participants who dominate the discussion.
  Sorry, Dieter, would you let Sophie finish her point?
- Make small talk before the meeting starts.
  Have you been to Paris before?
- Check the other participants have understood you.
  Has everyone understood me so far? If not, please let me know.
- Check you have understood the other participants.
  Let me just check that I have understood you correctly.
- Summarise frequently.
  Let me just quickly summarise what we have agreed so far.

■ Set up the meetings roleplay and designate one learner to be the chairperson. During the activity, listen and make notes for later feedback on errors and language which can be improved. Also, give the chairperson feedback on *their* performance and ask the other learners to comment.

Review Make cards based on what the learners need to do when managing international meetings. Give them out. Explain that during a roleplay they have to use all their cards – using a standard phrase for interrupting, etc.

Worksheet A

Steve from Detroit (age 26) asked the following question:

Last month I led my first international meeting. It took place in Europe and the participants were from Germany, France, Brazil and Japan. I prepared for the meeting as I would have in the States, but I didn't achieve the results that I wanted. Some of the participants came prepared to make decisions but others seemed only to want to discuss. Some openly gave their opinions but others didn't really participate.

The level of English of the participants was also really different. I had the feeling that some of my colleagues really didn't understand me. I thought that by the end of the meeting we had reached a decision and had put together an action plan, but now three weeks have passed and nothing has happened.

Could you give me some advice on managing international meetings? I have to lead one again in June and want to improve my performance.

Worksheet B

Bob, a top manager, replied to Steve's message:

Remember cultural differences when chairing international meetings!

It is really important to state clearly the expected outcome at the beginning of the meeting – to have a discussion, to make a decision, to share information – as different cultures might have different expectations about what happens in a meeting.

You also need to say how you intend to achieve this outcome – Will there be a vote? Will participants be expected to go back to their teams and report on the meeting? Will there be action points to be followed up?

There are lots of differences in communication styles, so make sure that you allow all participants the opportunity to take part in the discussion. You may need to ask some their opinion and stop others if they are dominating the proceedings.

No matter what cultures you are working with, making small talk before the meeting starts can help to create positive relationships, but keep it short and don't let it distract anyone from the purpose of the meeting.

Finally, think about the English that you use if you are dealing with non-native speakers. Make sure you do not use slang or idioms, and regularly check that the others have understood you. Check that you have understood what the participants are saying by asking questions and summarising their point.

Good luck in your next international meeting!

Cultural differences

Principle Learners need to be aware of how their cultural background affects how they behave in meetings – How might *their* behaviours differ from those of their business partners? Do this activity with groups of learners from a variety of different cultures (but it does also work well with homogenous groups).

Prepare
Make two copies of the observation sheet opposite for every three or four learners in the group. You will also need a case study to discuss (perhaps from a business English coursebook or resource pack).

Proceed
■ Put the learners into small groups, ideally, each one consisting of learners from one cultural background. Give each group a copy of the worksheet and ask them to discuss the questions and make notes. Set a time limit, then ask them to put their worksheets to one side.

■ Assign one person in each group to be the observer. Give this person the second copy of the worksheet and tell them that the other learners are going to take part in a meeting. Their task is to take notes on the questions as they observe what happens.

■ Give out copies of your case study (the observer should also get one, so that they know the context). Give the learners time to prepare it and then set a time limit for the discussion.

■ When they have finished discussing, get the observers to comment.

■ Return to the original worksheets and compare how the learners behaved in this meeting with their cultural expectations – Would they make any changes to what they originally wrote?

Alternative If teaching heterogeneous groups, get the learners to discuss the cultural differences that they noted. If not, elicit differences they have noted in meetings they have taken part in with different companies.

Large groups Pin the worksheets on the wall and get the learners to circulate and read what the other groups wrote.

Follow-up Get the learners to write a *Dos* and *Don'ts* list for taking part in meetings in their culture.

Cultural differences	Observations
Participation 1 Is everyone encouraged to participate in meetings? If so, how? 2 Is one person allowed to dominate the meeting?	
Conflict 1 Does conflict occur in meetings? Or is there an emphasis on consensus? 2 How is agreement/disagreement expressed?	
Communication 1 Is it considered acceptable to interrupt someone who is speaking? 2 What is the role of silence? Is it used to express agreement or disagreement? 3 Can you think of examples of non-verbal signals (eg nodding, for agreement)?	
Decisions 1 Are decisions made by the group or the individual? 2 Which of the following factors do the managers take into consideration when making decisions? • Financial gains • Concern for employees • Concern for the community • Concern for customers • Legal obligations • Corporate image/reputation	

Conference calls

Principle Learners need to transfer their own experience of telephone conferencing to telephone conferences in English. Reassure them that the rules and many of the difficulties are the same – basically, conference calls are meetings at a distance.

Prepare

Make a copy of the handout opposite for each learner in the group.

Proceed

■ Set the scene: the learners are talking to a new colleague who has just started in their department. The colleague asks for some advice on telephone conferencing – they are involved in one the next day but have no experience.

■ Put the learners into pairs and ask them to write a list of ten tips to help their colleague.

■ Give out the handout. Ask the learners to read it and compare the tips with their own ideas. Every company will have slightly different ways of doing things and their own set procedures, so the learners may well find some points they don't agree with. Get them to discuss the differences with their partner.

Follow-up You can do any meeting roleplay. Make sure that your learners are sitting in a circle with their backs to each other to simulate the lack of visual support of a conference call. If you have telephone conference facilities where you teach, use these to make the activity even more realistic.

Before the roleplay, make sure the learners follow the tips as they prepare. And as the conference takes place, use the tips yourself as a checklist to monitor and give feedback at the end.

Planning

- Make sure everyone gets the agenda before the conference call and looks through it.
- Think about time zones when planning the time of an international telephone conference. Make sure it is clear which time zone you mean when agreeing times and dates.
- A telephone conference typically takes longer than a face-to-face meeting, so plan accordingly.
- Make sure the telephone conference is not too long. A maximum of one hour is best.
- Ensure all participants have the dial-in number and pass-codes. Be clear about international dialling codes.
- Make sure you have a chairperson, although this does not have to be the same person who sets up the technical details of the call.
- Call from a quiet location, using a good-quality phone – not a cordless phone or a mobile phone, if possible.

Starting the call

- The chairperson should dial in early and be the first online.
- The chairperson should greet people by name as they dial in.
- Once everyone is available, the chairperson starts the meeting.

During the call

- Everyone should announce their name before speaking.
- Do not try to multi-task. Concentrate on the telephone conference. Don't check your emails or try to do other work.
- Announce if you are leaving or returning to the telephone conference.
- Speak clearly and slowly. Make sure you ask people to explain if you don't know what they mean.
- The chairperson should make sure everyone has the chance to speak, using people's names to get their attention.
- The chairperson should summarise each item before moving on to the next and give everyone the opportunity to ask questions.
- Finish on time.

After the call

- Distribute the minutes as soon as possible to all participants.

Opening statements

Principle Learners need to feel confident at the start of a negotiation, to have a better chance of success. Prepare and practise 'openings' where they state their aims and interest – to help them to feel less nervous.

Prepare
Prepare flipchart paper or OHTs.

Proceed
■ Write 'Opening statement' on the board/flipchart. Elicit what it normally includes and write ideas up – include what the negotiator would like to discuss and what their aims are.

■ Emphasise that it is important for learners to prepare an opening statement before a negotiation, especially when negotiating in a foreign language, and why.

■ Set up a 'negotiation' roleplay situation. Use the one below or create your own based on the learners' jobs.

> You are meeting the manager of a language school to negotiate English courses for your company. Use the notes below to prepare an opening statement.
>
> - Your company just merged with a company in the UK.
> - Administration staff need to be able to communicate more effectively with staff in the UK.
> - You think that telephoning and emailing are the most important skills to focus on.
>
> **Sample answer** We would like to discuss our language training needs. Our company has just merged with a company in the UK. Therefore, we would like to start offering English courses to our administration staff so they can better communicate with staff there. The courses should focus on telephoning and email skills. We are looking for a partner who will help us meet this need.

■ Put the learners into groups of two or three. Get them to write their 'statement of interest' on flipchart paper or an OHT. Monitor and check for accuracy.

■ Get them to take turns practising their statement of interest. At first, they read it out but as they practise it more and more, get them to learn it or use prompt cards – writing down only key phrases to help them memorise the whole statement.

Lower levels Give the learners sentence starters to complete:
- *We are here to discuss …*
- *The most important thing for us is …*
- *We are looking for …*

Focus on phases

Principle Learners need to think about the phases of a negotiation and become familiar with standard phrases for each one. Do this activity as an introduction to a series of 'negotiations' lessons or a negotiations workshop.

Prepare
Make a copy of the 'car purchasing' worksheet below for each learner.

Stage	What is done
Preparation	Research different models on the internet and in newspapers; decide how much to pay.
Establishing rapport	Go to the car dealer. Introduce yourself to the salesperson. Make small talk to establish a good relationship.
Discussion	Tell the salesperson what you are looking for and discuss what cars are available that would meet your needs. Get more information about cars that you could imagine buying.
Proposing	The salesperson tells you a price for a car that you are interested in buying.
Bargaining	Try to get the price down.
Settling	Agree on the price and sign the contract.

Proceed
■ Ask the learners to imagine that they are going to buy a new car. Put them into groups of two or three to brainstorm the process of buying a car from a car dealer – *'First I would research different models, then I would … .'*

■ Write the six stages from the worksheet on the board/flipchart, or show them on an OHT/PowerPoint slide.

■ Elicit what the learners would do at each stage.

■ Give out the worksheet. Get the learners to compare the stages/process with theirs.

Business professionals Use the worksheet to talk about a recent negotiation: What happened at each stage?

One-to-one Begin by first eliciting the types of negotiations the learner takes part in and then use these negotiations to elicit the phases – as opposed to talking about buying cars! Or rewrite the conversations to make them more relevant to their job – HR, sales, whatever.

Review Write up dialogues related to negotiating for a car. The learners match the dialogue to the phases. This is a good way to check that they have understood the sequences.

Focus on phrases

Principle Learners need to be familiar with the standard phrases they can use in a negotiation so that they can concentrate on other skills, such as listening and thinking about how to reply. Do this activity as a follow-up to *Focus on phases* (page 77).

Prepare

Make a copy of the worksheet opposite for each learner and a set of the cards for every two learners.

Think of a negotiation situation relevant to your learners. For example:

- Between software developers and a customer wanting an upgrade to current software. The customer wants a short deadline but not to pay for extra staff.
- Between an employee and a boss. The employee wants to get a qualification which will help in their job. The boss thinks it is too expensive and will involve too much time away from work.

You might find it useful to put the situation on cards.

Proceed

■ Put the learners into pairs and give out the Negotiating stages worksheet and the Negotiating phrases cards. Get the pairs to match a phrase to a stage. Monitor to check they are correct.

■ Explain the negotiation situation, or give it out written on a card.

■ Get the learners to decide which phrases they want to use in the negotiation, using the cards for ideas.

■ The learners roleplay the situation, using the worksheets as support.

Alternative Instead of using cards, get the learners to watch a negotiation on DVD or on the internet (put 'negotiation + video' into a search engine to find examples). Get them to listen for phrases that are used for each phase and write them down on the worksheet.

Review Adapt the worksheet by having three columns:

- Negotiation phase
- What you do
- What you say

The learners brainstorm what they do in each phase and what they say – for *Establishing rapport*, they can write 'introduce yourself' and then brainstorm suitable phrases.

Negotiating stages worksheet

Establishing rapport
Discussing
Making a proposal
Bargaining
Settling

Negotiating phrases cards

It's good to see you again.	How was your flight?
Let's begin by discussing how we are going to proceed.	Can you start by telling us what you need?
Our main interest is …	We are also interested in … . However, that isn't a main priority right now.
We propose a delivery date of July 11th. How does that sound to you?	Actually, we would prefer July 5th.
If you gave us a discount, we would consider a larger order.	Would you be willing to order more units if we lowered the price?
Can you be a bit more flexible with price? Then we would consider a larger order.	We could agree on that.
Let me just summarise what we have agreed.	We will send you a written agreement in a few days.

Question relay

Principle Learners need to be able to find out more details in a negotiation by asking questions themselves, as well as being able to handle their negotiating partner's questions. Follow this procedure as preparation for taking part in a negotiating roleplay.

Prepare

Prepare two 'opening statements' for a negotiation roleplay, one from a supplier and the other from a buyer. They can be based on *Focus on phrases* on page 78 or on the learners' jobs. Also, prepare the 'Questions' worksheet opposite and some sample answer cards for every two learners in the group.

Proceed

■ Put the learners into pairs. Give out the questions worksheet and the answer cards. Ask them to sort the questions from a negotiation into the correct categories. Monitor the answers, then tell them to think of one more question for each category. Check their answers are accurate and appropriate.

■ Dictate the 'opening statements'. The learners write, then compare and check back with you.

■ For each statement of interest, they write down one question they would ask the other party. When they have finished, they pass their question to the person sitting next to them.

■ They then write down a second question. Tell them they cannot write the same question as before, nor a question that is already on the piece of paper.

■ After writing a second question, the learners pass on the piece of paper again. Repeat the process until there are five or six questions on each piece of paper.

■ Monitor, check the questions and give feedback on any language issues – accuracy, directness, etc.

■ Put the learners into pairs and get them to do the roleplay, using the appropriate prepared questions. If there is time, get them to change partners and do the roleplay again, exchanging roles.

Questions worksheet

Direct questions	Indirect questions
Clarifying questions	Checking that the questioner is satisfied
Avoiding giving an answer	

Answer cards

When can you deliver the product?	Could you tell me more about what your expectations are?
Would you mind telling me more about your needs?	Could you explain that again, please?
Do you mean …?	Could we talk about that next time?
I am sorry but I don't have the figures with me right now.	Can you pay in 60 days?

Be prepared!

Principle Learners need to spend time preparing adequately before a negotiation. Give them the chance to prepare together as a team and think about the language that they want to use – as well as providing additional fluency practice.

Prepare
Make a copies of the worksheet opposite. You will also need to prepare (or get your learners to write) a negotiation roleplay.

Proceed
- Explain the negotiation. Give the learners the details and their roles, if necessary.
- Put them into two groups and give each group a copy of the worksheet.
- Get them to discuss the questions, using the negotiation roleplay as a basis for the answers. Set a time limit.
- Ask the learners to brainstorm vocabulary and functional phrases that they need for the negotiation – and then begin to negotiate.

Business professionals Instead of using the worksheet, elicit how *they* prepare for negotiations, coming up with a list of questions for the group to discuss before the negotiation starts. Get one of the learners to write the questions on the board so that the group can refer to them. Also get each learner to write down three or four phrases that they want to use in the negotiation.

Pre-experience learners If necessary, give additional background information before they begin to answer the questions on the worksheet. Spend some time talking about how good negotiators prepare for a negotiation, emphasising the importance of having clear objectives and considering the other party's objectives and needs.

One-to-one Give the learner time to jot down answers to the questions and then go through them together. After that focus on vocabulary specific to the negotiations that they take part in. To do this, it is helpful to go through work documents, such as agendas or contracts.

Learner autonomy Encourage business professionals to use the worksheet when preparing for real negotiations in English. For the vocabulary section, get them to go through work documents and note *new* vocabulary or vocabulary that they would *like* to use in their negotiation.

Negotiation preparation
Discuss these questions with the other members of your group:

1 What are the main issues and problems?

2 What are your main objectives?

3 What do you know about the other party?

4 How could you persuade the other party to move towards what you want?

5 For what reasons might the other party disagree with your proposals?

6 What common interests might you share?

Vocabulary
Write down the main topics that will be discussed during the negotiation. What vocabulary will you need for each topic?

Topic 1:

Topic 2:

Topic 3:

Phrases
Write down some phrases you want to use during the negotiation in order to do the following:

Establish rapport:

State your objectives:

Make a proposal:

Settle:

Clarify and check:

That's too late!

Principle Learners need to maintain a good relationship with their negotiating partner, but still get what they want. Emphasise and practise diplomatic language for the bargaining phase of a negotiation.

Prepare

Make a copy of the dialogue and of the cards opposite for every two learners, and make another copy of the dialogue for each learner. Also, think of a situation relevant to your learners. See the suggestions in *Focus on phrases* (page 78).

Proceed

■ Tell the learners they are going to read a conversation which takes place at a negotiation between a customer and a supplier discussing a new order. Elicit things that might be talked about (price, quantity, delivery dates).

■ Give out the dialogue and ask the learners to read it to see if their predictions were correct.

■ Ask them if they notice any impolite language. Put them into pairs to underline phrases in the dialogue which they think could be more diplomatic.

■ Now give out the cards and get the pairs to match the undiplomatic examples from the dialogue with a better version. Monitor to check they are matching correctly.

■ Once the cards are matched, elicit a few examples of how to make language diplomatic – 'softeners', indirect questions, etc.

■ Dictate some undiplomatic phrases:
- *I don't agree.*
- *That's not helpful.*
- *That's not possible.*

■ With their partner, the learners check the phrases then make them more diplomatic.

■ Explain the negotiation situation or give it to them on a card. In pairs, they write a short dialogue using diplomatic language for this situation. Set a time limit of up to ten minutes, then get the pairs to read out their dialogues or to exchange with another pair and read theirs.

Alternative Write your own dialogue, based on a situation closer to one your learners might find themselves in.

Follow-up Record the learners doing the negotiation, to analyse how good their intonation is. A wider intonation range helps make language more polite.

Higher levels Get the learners to roleplay a situation rather than write a dialogue. Give them a few minutes to prepare.

One-to-one You take the role of a very aggressive negotiating partner – the learner has to stay diplomatic at all costs!

Negotiating dialogue

A: Hello, Mr Brown. I'm sorry I'm late, I got stuck in traffic. I hope you still have time to see me.
B: I have another meeting to go to after this. We'll still have to finish at 11:00.
A: That should be OK. Did you get the chance to read the brochures I sent you?
B: Yes, but they weren't very helpful. You'll have to explain the procedure to me.
A: No problem.
B: It says here that we can only order in quantities of 1,000. We don't need that many. We only want 700.
A: That might be possible but it would affect the price.
B: No. We can't pay more.
A: Then you could order 1,000 and keep the rest in stock.
B: No. Our warehouse isn't big enough.
A: How about if we sent them in two deliveries.
B: That sounds better. When can you make the first delivery?
A: In four weeks.
B: That's too late. I need them in three weeks.
A: I'll have to check the factory schedule and get back to you.

Negotiating cards

We'll still have to finish at 11.00.	Would it be OK if we still finished at 11.00?
They weren't very helpful.	They didn't answer all my questions.
You'll have to explain the procedure to me.	I think you'll have to explain the procedure to me.
We don't need that many.	We don't really need that many.
We only want 700.	We were thinking of 700.
No. We can't pay more.	I'm afraid we can't pay more.
No. Our warehouse isn't big enough.	Unfortunately, our warehouse isn't big enough.
When can you make the first delivery?	Do you know when you can make the first delivery?
That's too late.	That would be too late.
I need them in three weeks.	I hoped to have them in three weeks.

Socialising quiz

Principle Learners need to know standard phrases for socialising with business partners. Diagnose first which functional phrases they already know.

Prepare

Make a copy of the quiz below for each learner in the group, leaving plenty of space for them to write.

What can you say?
1 You want to introduce yourself to a business partner for the first time.
2 You want to introduce your colleague to a business partner.
3 You want someone to use your first name.
4 A colleague just told you that she got a big promotion.
5 A colleague just told you that her mother is very ill.
6 You want to change the topic of conversation.
7 You want to end a conversation with someone who won't stop talking.
8 You want to say goodbye to someone you have met several times before.
9 You want to say goodbye to someone you just met for the first time.

Proceed

■ Ask the learners about situations where they socialise.

■ Put them into pairs and give out the copies of the quiz. Tell them to think of at least one phrase for each situation. Monitor, check the phrases are correct and help out if necessary.

■ Get the learners to highlight phrases on the quiz they could use in the situations – the ones they mentioned.

■ Ask them to choose four or five situations that are most relevant to their business situations. In pairs, they practise these situations. Monitor and give feedback.

Business professionals Make the quiz specific to a context in which you know they actually make small talk – in a restaurant (offering to pay the bill) or before a meeting (finding out if their business partner would like a coffee).

Learner autonomy Put the situations onto cards. Elicit phrases for each situation or write them on the board. The learners write the phrases that they would like to learn on the cards. This will make it easy for them to review the language out of the lesson.

First impressions count

Principle Learners need to be able to make a positive first impression when meeting business partners. Teach functional phrases for starting conversations.

Prepare

Find a picture of two business people shaking hands. You can find one on the internet or in a magazine. Put it on an OHT or use PowerPoint – or make photocopies.

Proceed

■ Elicit why first impressions are important – when business people have little time and make decisions quickly, personal relationships are very important.

■ Show the learners your picture and tell them that these people are meeting at a conference for the first time. Ask where *they* meet people for the first time and elicit how they might start the conversation:
>   A: *Hello, I'm … from …*
>   B: *Nice to meet you. I'm … from …*

■ Elicit questions that the two people in the picture may ask:
>   *What exactly does your company do?*
>   *And what do you do?*
>   *What are you responsible for?*

■ Get them individually to write short but full answers to the following questions for their own jobs:
>   *We make …*
>   *We source our products …*
>   *We're currently planning to …*
>   *I'm responsible for …*
>   *I work very closely with …*
>   *I've been doing this job now for …*

■ In pairs, they should introduce themselves and find out something about their partner's job. Monitor and make a note of any errors, for feedback at the end.

■ Get the learners to find a new partner and practise the dialogue again.

■ Ask them to perform their roleplays to the rest of the group. The audience has to comment: Did they make a good impression? Or not?

Qualification seekers Practise the language in an exam situation. You take the role of the examiner.

Pre-experience learners Change the context so that it takes place at a job fair – they practise describing their studies. Or they describe their preferred *future* jobs.

Learner autonomy Ask them to note on a framework language that they will want to use when socialising, for future revision on their own.

Keep it going

Principle Learners need to be able to make small talk to build relationships. Stop conversation becoming a series of questions and single-word answers, by teaching strategies for reacting to what the other person has said.

Prepare

Prepare a 'bad' and a 'good' conversation. Make photocopies of the conversations for every two learners in the group.

Proceed

■ Put the learners into pairs and give them a copy of the bad conversation. Get them to discuss the dialogue, decide what is wrong with it and suggest improvements.

■ Give out the good conversation and get them to compare the two versions: What makes the second one better?

■ Get the learners to analyse the second conversation:
  • Underline any phrases used to react to what the other person said – *It was great.*
  • Highlight phrases referring to future action – *I'll …*

■ In feedback, check the analysis and expand further:
  • How the speakers react to the questions then expand with further details – *Yes, I heard that* (reaction). *I had a call from Sylvie* (further details).
  • How Speaker B asks Speaker A a follow-up question on the same subject – *Have you ever been to the Paris office?*
  • How Speaker A asks a question on a completely different subject – *By the way, …*

■ Get the learners to decide on two general topics and to make small talk for at least two minutes. Tell them to use as many phrases as possible from the previous steps and to ask follow-up questions. You could set one person the task of listening and noting down how many of the phrases, and how many follow-up questions, they used.

Higher levels Put the learners into pairs and ask them to come up with alternatives to some underlined phrases:
> It was great: *it was fine/good/really productive/interesting/really useful*
> Yes, I heard that: *So I heard; Yes, Sylvie told me that.*
> Yes, and: *Yes, it was; Yes, I thought …*

One-to-one In one lesson, make a recording of you and the learner making small talk. Between lessons, transcribe the conversation then rewrite it to improve it. Show both versions to the learner and elicit the differences.

Learner autonomy More vocabulary and more ready-made word associations make it easier to keep conversations going. Learners can use mindmaps like the one opposite to increase their range (see programs such as www.bubbl.us).

Bad conversation

A: Hi Bob, how was your trip to the Paris office?
B: Fine.
A: I had a call from Sylvie saying the meeting was good.
B: Oh.
A: What time is the team meeting this afternoon?
B: I don't know.
A: OK. Bye.

Good conversation

A: Hi Bob, how was your trip to the Paris office?
B: It was great. We made a lot of progress on the new guidelines for the X3 project.
A: Yes, I heard that. I had a call from Sylvie saying the meeting was good.
B: Yes, and it was good to meet her face-to-face after having spoken to her on the phone so many times.
A: I know what you mean. By the way, what time is the team meeting this afternoon?
B: I'm not sure. I'll ask Frank and give you a call when I find out.
A: Thanks. Speak to you later.
B: Bye.

Conversation mindmap

Conversation exchange

Principle Learners need to practise using socialising language in situations that are realistic for them. Keep adding new language to a worksheet every time you focus on socialising during the course.

Prepare

Make a copy of the worksheet for each learner in the group.

Greetings and introductions	Introducing your colleagues
Reacting to good news	Reacting to bad news
Changing the topic of a conversation	Ending a conversation and saying goodbye

Have ready a pile of blank index cards.

Proceed

■ Put the learners into pairs, give out the worksheet and get them to come up with two or three phrases for each category. Monitor to check the phrases are correct, giving suggestions and correcting and practising pronunciation.

■ Give the learners some blank cards to write a socialising situation, thinking of *where* and *who* they will socialise with:

> **Place:** a restaurant in Moscow
> **People:** a very important customer

■ Collect the cards, shuffle and deal them out so that every pair has some. Get the learners to decide which phrases they want to use in their conversation.

■ They roleplay a short conversation and each time they use one of the phrases they mark it off their list. When they have finished their cards, they exchange with another pair.

Alternative Use a short video clip – eg a TV programme – where characters make small talk. Type up a transcript. After watching together, give out the script and get the learners to underline phrases that match the functions on your worksheet. Check, and then get them to transfer the phrases that they want to learn onto the worksheet.

Review Keep the cards. In the next lesson, pass them out and quickly elicit a phrase or phrases that the learners can use in each one.

Conversation cards

Principle Learners need to practise making small talk on topics that they consider relevant and interesting. Use cards again and again to practise socialising language.

Prepare

Make a set of conversation cards for every two or three learners. You will probably want to add to these or leave some out, depending on your learners.

Sport	Weather	The journey
Your hotel	Local food	Politics
Religion	Fashion	Shopping
Places to eat	Hobbies	Family
Interesting things to do in this town	Personal appearance	People you both know

Proceed

■ Put the learners into pairs and give them a set of cards. Ask them to divide the cards into four categories:
- *Boring*
- *Interesting*
- *Safe*
- *Taboo*

■ Elicit their categories and write them up on the board/flipchart. Allow time for discussion.

■ Ask – *Which topics would you speak about with your business partners?* Again, allow time for discussion. Circle the topics that they consider the most relevant or interesting for their particular situations.

■ Put the learners into groups of two or three. Tell them to 'small talk' about the topics that are circled on the board.

■ Monitor carefully, noting good language and areas where the learners can improve, to help planning future lessons.

Alternative Give two or three *blank* cards to each learner and get them to write one small talk topic on each. These could be topics from the news or from the company. Brainstorm vocabulary for each topic and then get the learners to practise small talk based on their topics.

One-to-one Record the small talk conversation with your learner and listen to it together. Give feedback on what they did well and where improvements could be made. Then record and listen again, to notice improvements.

Review Play a game. Give each learner one card. Tell them that they have to make small talk about the card but they can't say the word on the card. Set a time limit. The others have to guess which cards they had.

Listening actively

Principle Learners need to develop their 'active listening' skills as well as their speaking, as a way of maintaining a conversation. Focus on strategies such as as body language, summarising, questioning and back-channelling devices (*yeah, I see, oh*).

Prepare
Prepare some cards (see *Conversation cards* on page 84).

Proceed
- Choose one learner to be your 'small talk' partner and invite them to the front of the class.

- Tell the others to note the strategies that you use to keep the conversation going.

- Make small talk for two or three minutes, using lots of active listening strategies to get the learner to keep talking.

- Elicit the strategies you used and write them on the board/flipchart – phrases the learners can use for summarising, and questions for showing interest. Write these up as well.

- Put the learners into pairs, specifying who is A and who is B, and give each pair a conversation card. Tell them to make small talk until you say 'Stop'. Learner A has to summarise what Learner B said, then ask a question which will encourage them to continue from where they left off. If necessary, demonstrate this with a volunteer:
    A: *My last holiday was March last year when I went to Australia. I went there with my boyfriend and we flew to Sydney first of all, which was …*
    Teacher: *Stop!*
    B: *So you went to Australia last March with your boyfriend and you started in Sydney. Did you like it there?*
    A: *Yes, it was great. We did so many things – we went on the ferry to the beach, we got a train into the Blue Mountains, we …*
    Teacher: *Stop!*
    B: *So you went to the beach and some mountains. What were they called again?*
    A: *The Blue Mountains.*

- Monitor and give feedback.

Alternative Make it into a competition. The group that can talk the longest about one topic wins.

One-to-one Make a recording of the two of you making small talk. Listen to the recording and elicit strategies that you used to keep the learner talking. Then make a second recording, urging them to use the same strategies. Listen again and assess improvement.

Socialising internationally

Principle Learners need to be aware of how socialising customs in their country may differ from those of their business partners. Allow a lot of time for discussions like this – they work particularly well with heterogeneous groups, as they can talk about differences between their cultures.

Prepare
Prepare a questionnaire on cultural differences:

> In your country …
> - Is it typical for business to take place over a meal?
> - Is it common to invite business people to your home?
> - Is it usual to provide international guests with entertainment in the evening?
> - Is it normal to make small talk at the start of a telephone conversation?
> - How much time is spent making small talk at the start of a meeting?
> - What are common small talk topics?

Make a copy for each learner in the group.

Proceed
- Put the learners into small groups and give them the questionnaire.

- Ask them to read the questions and think about their answers individually for a few minutes, then discuss in groups. Set a time limit, but allow plenty of time for discussion before getting the learners to share their ideas with the whole group.

Business professionals Get them to discuss a country which they travel to for their jobs and give advice to their course colleagues.

Homework Ask the learners to research a particular country, using the internet. They can then report back at the beginning of the next lesson

How interesting!

Principle Learners need to be able to react appropriately to information that their business partners give them. Give them the confidence to use intonation patterns correctly.

Prepare
Make copies of the 'reaction' and 'situation' cards for every two learners in the group.

Proceed

■ Put the learners into pairs, give out the *reaction* cards and ask them to sort them into two piles – positive and negative.

■ Give out the *situation* cards. Get the pairs to decide on a suitable reaction for each card. (There may be more than one possibility.)

■ Demonstrate how intonation patterns can add meaning to the phrases. Use one of the example pairs of cards the learners have chosen (*I've just bought a new car*). Say *That's fantastic!* with a very wide intonation range, so that you sound really pleased.

■ Now say it with a flat intonation range – as if you aren't really interested.

■ Ask the learners to explain exactly how you made the phrases sound different, then get them to practise the phrase with their partners, sounding excited and uninterested in turns.

■ They take a piece of paper and imagine that their colleague has just got back from a three-week holiday. They note down things that happened meanwhile:
  - One really good thing
  - One quite good thing
  - One quite bad thing
  - One really bad thing

■ Get the learners to tell their partners one of their ideas (in no particular order) and their partner chooses a phrase to react:
  A: *The coffee machine broke.*
  B: *Oh no!*
  A: *My boss told me I can have two weeks off this summer.*
  B: *That's fantastic!*

■ Monitor and give feedback, focusing on intonation.

Review In pairs, get the learners to decide on two or three small talk topics. Give one learner a *review* card like the ones opposite and tell them to use a suitable intonation. Get them to have a conversation while their partner tries to guess what is on the card.

Reaction cards

That's fantastic.	That's great.	That's wonderful.
That's really good.	That's interesting.	That's nice.
That's not so good.	Oh no!	That's really bad.
That's terrible.	That's awful.	I'm sorry to hear that.

Situation cards

I've just bought a new car.	I've won the lottery.	I'm getting married.
I found 50 Euros in the street.	I've just booked a holiday to the Caribbean.	I can't remember my password for my PC.
My PC just crashed and I hadn't saved my document.	My boss wants a serious talk with me this afternoon.	I crashed my car on the way to work today.
My dog was killed by a car yesterday.	I just got a 500 Euro mobile phone bill for this month.	I saw a really good film last night.
Now I'd like to look at …	Let's move on to …	Turning to …
I've lost my mobile phone.	I'm going to try out a new restaurant this weekend.	I fell down the stairs yesterday and broke my leg.

Review cards

a bit interested	very interested	angry
bored	surprised	horrified

Chapter 3
The business of language

- Frameworks
- Authentic/work materials
- Vocabulary
- Phonology
- Grammar

Frameworks

What are they? A framework is a worksheet with space for the learners to add their own ideas and information. It is typically used to brainstorm before a speaking activity or to begin a discussion. Frameworks are ideal for speaking skills and fluency practice.

What are the benefits? They provide guidance and structure for learners in speaking activities – especially for those who say that they 'just want to talk' in their lessons.

- Essentially, they are blank worksheets – yet they match some learners' expectations much more than if the teacher just 'chats'.
- Very learner-centred – all the information comes from the learners, removing the risk that they will not find interesting the material you have provided.
- Flexible – they can be the basis for a long discussion, yet demand little preparation.
- A vehicle for the teacher – or other group members – to find out more about a learner's personal work situation and opinions.
- Good support for visual learners – who expect to be provided with something 'to look at'.

Where can I get them? There are some resource files of photocopiable frameworks on the market but they are also extremely easy to create yourself. (See the sample lesson plans in the 'Frameworks' section, although many other activities in this book include frameworks.)

How can I use them? Frameworks give support in a discussion activity.

- Working individually: they help the learners to brainstorm opinions or facts, or to organise their thoughts before discussing with another learner – or with the teacher in the case of a one-to-one learner.
- In pairs: they help them to prepare before they present their ideas to the rest of the group or to another pair.

Who can I use them with? With all your learners. Lower levels gain confidence by having time to prepare and check the language they need for an activity. Advanced levels discuss and experiment with vocabulary and structures, and have the opportunity to speak at length.

Authentic/work materials

■ What are authentic materials?
News articles and podcasts, etc, which were not produced specifically for teaching and learning English. They are ideal for practising reading and listening skills.

What are the benefits? They present the learners with real-life language:

- A rich source of vocabulary – including collocations, idioms and phrasal verbs.
- Reading and listening practice – in motivating and realistic contexts.
- They lead to interesting discussions which help the learners develop their fluency skills – asking for and giving opinions.
- They can also be used for grammar work – revealing how certain structures are used in a real (rather than specially written) text.

Where can I get them? You can use print newspapers or magazines, or the online versions (the advantage here is that you can cut and paste the text into a word processor to manipulate it – putting in gaps or cutting it up into different parts). Check the company websites of places where you teach:

- Many of these have a press area where you can find any recent articles published about the company.
- They are a rich resource – mission statements, jobs, official statements from the board and many other real and interesting items. Other company resources might be leaflets and brochures or other sales material, promotional videos and presentations.

How can I use them? The basic format can be the same for *any* reading or listening lesson which you are used to:

- **Before** Prediction.
- **During** Work-related activities – to make the most of the genuine interest generated by the predictions.
  - Timed – to encourage skimming through the text for meaning without worrying too much about unknown vocabulary.
  - Tasks – *Were the predictions right? What is their opinion? What would they do?*
  - Pairwork – followed by plenary discussion.
- **After** – Consolidation.

The business of language

■ What are work materials?

These are documents or materials that learners may actually produce, use and need to understand for their jobs – promotional brochures/flyers/videos, advertisements, manuals, minutes and agendas, emails, contracts, action plans, reports, company websites, presentations, financial statements. They are ideal for reading and writing skills.

What are the benefits? Using work documents makes lessons immediately relevant to the needs of your business professionals:

- If they write emails (which is not unlikely!) the best starting point is with some emails they have already written.
- If they give presentations in English, it is more authentic to use one of those presentations for practice.

Use work documents when teaching writing skills, because the format and style of documents will be different in every company – possibly every department – and by focusing on the learners' own work you can identify their own areas for development. They are an excellent source of language, as well as being useful for giving the learners opportunities to use work-related vocabulary:

- Agendas generate vocabulary for meetings.
- Promotional brochures generate vocabulary for product presentations.
- Financial statements generate vocabulary for company reports.

What do I need to do? Get a commitment from the learners to provide you with documents that they use for their jobs.

- They should give you the materials in advance so you have time to prepare – they can't bring material to class and expect to work with it immediately.
- The documents should be in English and that they should not expect you to translate them.
- They cannot expect you to translate English documents into their native language for them.

Make your activities relevant to what they really do with the documents. Ask questions about the materials:

- Why do they want to look at this in class?
- In what ways is the material interesting/useful?
- What is it they need to do?
  - Read and understand?
  - Write in this style?
  - Reply to this?
  - Learn the vocabulary?
  - Discuss the content?

Remember: Don't pretend that you are an expert if you are not. Work-related documents are often difficult to understand if you are from outside the company or department. If you are unfamiliar with the content, get the learners to explain it – this gives them fluency practice and enables them to practise work-related vocabulary.

Vocabulary

What kind of vocabulary do business learners need?
They need *general* business vocabulary to be able to talk about the everyday aspects of working life – going to meetings, describing different departments in the company. However, they also need *specialist* vocabulary:

- Related to their industry – financial terms for a banker, the names of machine parts for an engineer
- Related to their company – very company-specific job titles or other terms

Specialist vocabulary can also include academic terms – scientists who need to write up reports on their work.

How do I teach vocabulary? All vocabulary, specialised and general, is made up of different types of words – including root words and other parts of speech in that word family (*compete, competition, competitor, competitive*). Vocabulary, however, is not always at the level of a single word – we cannot neglect idioms (*back to the drawing board*), compound nouns (*wastepaper bin*) and multi-word verbs (the meeting was *put back*).

Learners need to be made aware of the following:

- Style and register – Is it formal or informal? Old-fashioned or modern? Technical or in general use?
- Connotations – Is it positive or negative? Are there hidden meanings?
- Pronunciation – How is it said?
- Grammar – Where does it go in the sentence? How are the other parts of speech formed?
- Collocations – What are its 'partners'? The word *meeting* is often teamed with the verbs *go to, attend, cancel, arrange*; with the adjectives *long, productive, quick*; with the nouns *department* and *sales*. A learner who *declines* a meeting instead of *cancelling* it is making a mistake in the partnership they choose.

Acquisition of new vocabulary is a process over time. Before a learner really knows a word, they have to meet it many times in many different ways. Strategies need to be taught – how to learn it so they can develop their range on their own:

- Vocabulary always needs to be taught within a context, preferably your learners'.
- Lessons should contain production activities which include personalisation.
- Specialist vocabulary often cannot be found in coursebooks, TEFL internet sites or general English

dictionaries, so you have to rely on and exploit authentic materials, especially what the learners give you – emails, in-house magazines, annual reports, minutes.

- Many of the 'normal' criteria for selection are *not* relevant – how often the word occurs (frequency) and in which genres (range), availability (how readily it comes to mind), teachability (easy to illustrate meaning, concrete, related to other words) and learnability (no particular phonological/spelling difficulties).
- You may not have knowledge and understanding of the vocabulary yourself.

What if I don't know the terms? Be prepared to do a certain amount of background research yourself – using the internet, specialist dictionaries or resource books and talking to experienced colleagues. As you become more familiar with the learners and their company and gain more experience in different areas of business, this will become easier. But remember: use the *learners* as a resource.

- In company literature, they can identify vocabulary they want to learn and explain it to you from the context.
- One person in the group can explain the vocabulary to the others.

Do not be embarrassed about not knowing very specialised vocabulary – you are not expected to know legal terms if you are not a trained lawyer or technical parts for a machine if you are not an engineer. However, you should be aware of general vocabulary items connected with these areas and have an interest in, and willingness to learn about, more specialist areas.

Once the target vocabulary has been identified, teach the words in the same way you would general vocabulary words:

- Meaning, collocation, connotation, register, style, pronunciation and word grammar
- Learning strategies so that the learners can become more independent learners

So what can I focus on? It depends on the needs of the learners:

- Some need to spend time building up vocabulary in order to give presentations or to understand trade journals.
- Others have a good range of passive vocabulary but need practice in using the vocabulary actively and pronouncing it correctly.
- A one-to-one learner who has just taken on a new job in sales may have to learn vocabulary related to the product that they are selling.

How can I manage a mixed group? Imagine one of your groups has two engineers and three people from sales administration – they *all* want to learn vocabulary related to their job.

- If they are from the same company, there will be a certain amount of overlap – company structure, history, future plans, the industry in general.
- For more specific areas, speak to the learners and set priorities.
- Focus on strategies for learning vocabulary that equip them to use their own work-related documents as a resource for improving their own vocabulary.
- Give them opportunities to communicate in the lessons – talking about processes in their jobs, to personalise the vocabulary. And it can be very motivating for their colleagues to learn what someone else in the company does. A genuine information gap!

Phonology

What exactly does 'phonology' cover? Pronunciation is the way in which a word or language is pronounced. Phonology is the study of the pattern of speech sounds used in a particular language. We need to think about both – the pronunciation of individual sounds as represented by the symbols on the phonemic chart and the smallest parts into which a word can be broken down, but also:

- Intonation – where the voice rises and falls when speaking
- Word stress – which syllable is emphasised in a multi-syllabic word
- Sentence stress – which word is emphasised in a sentence
- Connected speech – how sounds change, are shortened or sometimes disappear altogether when words are spoken together in normal speech rather than in isolation
- Pauses – how speech is broken up to make phrases by pausing

Is it important? Phonology and pronunciation are integral to most business skills.

- In a meeting – to be understood by the other participants
- In a presentation – to keep the audience's interest and get a point across better by using appropriate intonation and pausing in the right places
- On the telephone – pronunciation is even more important when there is no extra-linguistic help such as facial gestures or body language

The business of language

However, you need to talk to your learners about their *targets* for pronunciation. Most learners do not want to or need to sound like a native speaker – their aim is to be understood. In fact, they often prefer to keep their own accent because it is part of their personal identity.

- Copying a native speaker model right down to the level of individual sounds might not be necessary – 'had' versus 'head' – because in context it would usually be clear which word the learner means.
- Training the learner to use features of connected speech may not be necessary in a context where only non-native speakers are using English to communicate.

How will I teach it? Many teachers automatically think about the phonemic chart. This is an extremely useful way of referring to the sounds of English. Copies can often be found on classroom walls and there are plenty available on the internet.

- Stress to learners that they do not have to learn all the symbols by heart – there are often words on the chart to help them remember what each symbol represents.
- The symbols are an aid to see how sounds can be the same even if spelling is different. In addition, the symbols and their sounds are in many learner dictionaries.

Phonology should be integrated into *all* your teaching – when teaching vocabulary and grammatical forms, the pronunciation of new words and structures is just as important as meaning, form and use.

- Record the learner in a meeting roleplay or a presentation then listen to it, paying particular attention to the intonation, pausing and sentence stress.
- Watch a professional presentation and analyse how that person uses their voice for effect – the learners can then try out some of the techniques.

Grammar

Is it important? How much grammar you teach and how you do it will depend on the learners. In business English, grammar is often integrated into skills lessons – the present continuous for future is often taught in a lesson on making arrangements on the telephone. There may be a more overt focus on grammar with lower levels, but higher levels still need to work on accuracy – if they speak to native speakers or write reports.

You will of course have a sound knowledge of the grammar systems of English. You may not teach 'grammar lessons' very often, but you need to be able to deal with questions from learners and give feedback on errors which arise because of problems with grammar.

What are the aims of a grammar lesson? If teaching lower levels, the aim may be to introduce and practise a new structure. With intermediate learners or above, it may be to focus on a structure that you have noticed is a 'problem area'. You could also focus on a structure that learners need for a particular business skill (the present perfect for talking about trends and figures, or the passive for describing processes).

How can I focus on grammar? Approaches in a business English classroom are similar to those in a general English classroom. One approach that works well is 'guided discovery' – giving learners language input and then getting them to work out 'rules' on their own. You can ask questions to guide them to the answers:

- Give them cards, some of which have sentences in the present simple – *The company produces automobiles* – and some have sentences in the present continuous – *The company is expanding in Asia right now.*
- They first sort the cards, considering differences in meaning, and then they focus on the form (third person -*s*, and verb + *ing*).

Another approach that works well is 'Test-Teach-Test'. A full example procedure is outlined on page 110.

What about practice? For business English learners, it is important that practice activities are personalised – that the activities are relevant to them, their job, company or business sector – even if you are just giving gapped sentences as controlled practice of a structure. Learners find this motivating, and it helps them to connect what they are doing in the classroom to the business world.

You can establish a context related to the learners' jobs in which the target language can be drawn out:

- Elicit what the learners do every day in their job.
- Write this on the board/flipchart as a mindmap.
- Get them to use what is written up to practise.

And there it is – the present simple meaningfully and, hopefully, memorably reviewed!

SWOT analysis

Principle Learners need to use work-related vocabulary in context and be able to talk about their company. Use a common business tool, the SWOT analysis framework, to prompt discussion about their place of work, highlighting lexis they lack while enabling you to learn more about their company and work situation – which will help make future lessons more relevant.

Prepare
Make a copy of a SWOT analysis framework for every two or three learners in the group.

Strengths	Weaknesses
Opportunities	Threats

Proceed
- Write SWOT on the board/flipchart. Tell the learners they are going to think of strengths, weaknesses, opportunities and threats for their company.
- Elicit one example of each category:
    Strength: brand new product
    Weakness: very expensive
    Opportunity: no one else has it
    Threat: competitors will copy it more cheaply
- Give out a SWOT analysis framework to each pair or small group. Tell them to think of as many 'swots' as possible for their company, and make notes.
- Monitor and provide vocabulary where needed. Note any errors worthy of comment.
- Give feedback on the language used and on any mistakes which need correcting.

Alternative Instead of analysing their company, the learners can talk about their department or a new business idea.

Pre-experience learners Get them to talk about a famous company or a product they all know.

Skills stategies

Principle Learners need to build up strategies to use in an exam, if they are seeking a qualification. Exam coursebooks normally include such tips and strategies throughout the book. Encourage the learners to record new tips on a single piece of paper, which they can easily refer to later in their exam preparation.

Of course, this framework doesn't have to be limited to exam preparation. You can get the learners to note general (as well as personalised) suggestions on all four skills throughout the course, for ongoing revision.

Prepare
Create a framework and make a copy for each learner.

Speaking	**Listening**
Strategy: *Clearly structure the presentation.*	Strategy: *Underline key words in the answers.*
Reading	**Writing**
Strategy:	Strategy:

Proceed
- At the beginning of the course, give each learner a copy of the framework. Tell them to store it in their binder so that they can easily find it – right at the front!
- At the end of each lesson, elicit tips that they learned for the exam and give them time to record these.

Follow-up Allow the learners to refer to the framework when they do practice exams. However, remind them that this will not be allowed when they do the real thing!

Review In the lesson before the exam, or before a practice exam, allow the learners to talk in pairs or small groups about what they have written on their frameworks. This will help them to reinforce what they have learned, as well as sharing their good ideas with their colleagues.

Grammar at work

Principle Learners need to be able to use a variety of tenses and aspects accurately. Although they can often do this in controlled-practice activities such as grammar gap-fills, they sometimes find it more difficult when concentrating on content. Do a free-practice activity after a grammar lesson on tenses – around a topic where everyone has an opinion.

Prepare
Make a copy of the framework for each learner in the group.

Past
Present
Future

Proceed
- Give an example of a change which has taken place in *your* job since you started – at first, listening activities were done using cassette players, now you use an MP3 player.

- Tell the learners they are going to think about changes in *their* jobs. Give out the framework and set them a time limit of three to five minutes to make notes: What changes have taken place in their job or workplace since they started? What do they think will happen in these areas?
  - Communication
  - Size of the company
  - Colleagues
  - Management
  - Products
  - Technology
  - Location
  - Customers
  - Suppliers

- Put the learners into pairs or small groups and get them to discuss, using the notes they have made.

- Monitor, help out with any necessary language and make notes of errors for feedback at the end.

Lower levels Make a version which concentrates only on past and present simple – *In 1990 we sent faxes, today we send emails.*

Higher levels Record the learners talking about changes in their jobs, then get them to listen and analyse the discussion for errors in tense use.

Review Use your feedback notes to decide which structures you need to work on in future lessons.

My last phone call

Principle Learners need to bring their work experience to lessons so that you can better help them transfer the language you teach to their jobs. Find out exactly what they do in English in a specific business skill (here, telephoning) – making the target language more relevant by personalising the subject area.

Prepare
Copy the framework for each learner. This example uses telephoning, but it can easily be adapted to any business skill.

What was it about?
Who did you talk to?
How long did it last?
Did you have any problems with your English?
How did you feel afterwards?

Proceed
- Give out the framework and tell the learners they have two or three minutes to think about their last phone call and make notes.

- Put them into pairs or small groups to tell each other about the last phone call they made. Encourage them to ask each other questions to find out more.

- Give feedback on the language they used and any errors which need correcting.

Alternative Other business subjects could be: 'my last email/meeting/presentation/business trip/negotiation' – or any other relevant skill or activity.

Lower levels Give extra support and supply missing language. The discussion stage will not take as long as with more advanced levels.

Homework Give a similar framework for the learners to fill in about a phone call (or other business activity) they will make between this lesson and the next. At the start of the next lesson, get them to report how it went.

Review Use the information you gain to inform future revision and planning.

The good manager

Principle Learners need to be able to express complex ideas on occasion. Use a framework with any learners in any context, discussing concepts like leadership – talking about the experience of *having* managers or talking from the point of view of *being* a manager.

Prepare
Make a copy of the framework for every two or three learners in the group.

> A good manager should …
>
> •
>
> •
>
> •
>
> •

Proceed
- Elicit a definition of a manager. This is not as easy as it sounds and may lead to a number of different opinions between the group members.

- Put the learners into pairs or small groups. Hand out the framework and ask them to decide things that a manager should be able to do. Set a time limit, perhaps ten minutes.

- Monitor during the activity, help out where language is needed and make notes of errors for feedback.

- Once the time limit is up, have a whole-group discussion to see if anyone had similar ideas or if they were all completely different. If the group is very large, form smaller groups containing people from different pairs.

- Finally, give feedback on the language the learners used and any errors which need correcting.

Follow-up Get the learners to think of appropriate *adjectives* to describe a good manager.

Lower levels Allow less preparation time for making notes on the framework, monitor and provide as much language as necessary.

Talking about processes

Principle Learners need to be skilled in describing processes – for example, business professionals involved in production who give tours around a factory. Help them to break things down into simple stages.

Prepare
Copy the framework for every two learners.

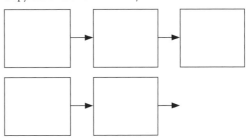

Proceed
- Choose a process which is fairly simple and which everyone will be familiar with. Draw some boxes and arrows on the whiteboard, as in the framework. (Alternatively, use an overhead projector and write directly onto the transparency.) A process for arranging the next English lesson might be:

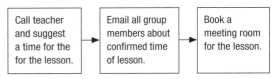

- Put the learners into pairs and get them to decide on a process they need to describe in their workplace.

- Hand out the framework. The pairs make notes about the different stages of the process.

- Get them to find new partners and tell each other about the processes they have described. Encourage them to ask each other questions to find out more.

- Give feedback on the language the learners used and any errors which need correcting.

Business professionals Get learners from different companies or different departments to work individually before telling their partner about their process. This can be an interesting way to learn how different companies do the same things in different ways.

Office-based workers Use this as a fluency activity – describing the process of putting in a holiday request form.

Review Repeat this activity in a lesson on passives and sequencing words (*Bottled!* on page 108).

Mixed learners, mixed tasks

Principle Learners need support when dealing with an authentic reading text. Provide differentiated help where some learners are low level and some know a lot more. A mixed-level group should exclude the use of authentic materials.

Prepare

Choose a reading text – a news article which you want to use in a lesson. Alternatively, get your learners to provide a text they are interested in discussing.

Prepare two sets of questions, one easier – true/false questions – and one more difficult – open comprehension questions. Make one copy of the text for each learner. Decide who will get each task and make a copy for them. Think of a follow-up discussion task.

Proceed

- Set up the reading task as usual with a prediction exercise.

- Give out the text to each learner and give out the different tasks as appropriate. Set a time limit.

- As the learners have completed different tasks, you will not be able to do any whole-group feedback, so make sure they compare their answers with someone who has done the same task. Monitor to check for any difficulties.

- Finish with a discussion. Tell the learners what the exact topic will be and give them time to prepare some things to say:
  - You can consider having them discuss in smaller groups made up only of higher or lower levels.
  - If you have everyone talking together, make one of the higher-level members a 'chairperson' who is responsible for making sure everyone has the chance to speak.

Alternative Use the higher-level learners to help *teach* the lower levels – while the latter are working on a very structured task, the higher levels can be working out and writing definitions for some vocabulary in the text, to then explain it to their colleagues. This is a very authentic task – learners very often find themselves in situations where their English is better than that of a colleague who they have to help out.

Company websites

Principle Learners need to develop skills in scanning long texts for specific information. Use company websites – they are also a great resource for topical news as well as company-specific vocabulary.

Prepare

Find the website of the company you are working in. The websites of international companies are usually in English as well as the local language.

Read the company information on the website and then prepare basic headings on a mindmap:

Make enough copies for each learner in the group.

This lesson works best if the learners have access to computers in the lesson. If not, print out the relevant information and make sufficient copies.

Proceed

- Put the learners into pairs and give each pair a copy of the mindmap. Get them to brainstorm what they know about the various headings.

- They present their ideas to the group and then look at the website to find missing information and to correct errors.

Business professionals Get them to read their company's internet site. If your learners' company does not have a website in English, you could look at those of their competitors, a similar company in an English-speaking country or a well-known international company.

Pre-experience learners Get them to read the internet site of a company they would like to work for.

Lower levels Give the learners true/false statements about the company, based on the web page. Get them to read the information and report back.

Large groups Use very detailed web pages, dividing the information into sections. Once this has all been collected, the whole group joins together to share their information.

Learner autonomy Remind them to read their company news in English on a regular basis to practise reading skills out of lessons.

Different points of view

Principle Learners need to develop skills in reading for detail. Encourage them to read a news article then to speak about it. This activity works well with higher-level learners – it involves different versions of the same story and creates a genuine information gap.

Prepare

Find two news articles which cover the same news story in two different newspapers or websites. Choose articles from newspapers with very different styles – a quality newspaper and a tabloid. Make enough copies so that half the learners have one and half have the other.

Proceed

- Put the learners into pairs and give each one of the pair a different article. They both make notes of the most important facts, either on a separate sheet of paper or by underlining/highlighting parts of the text. Set a time limit appropriate to the length of the articles.

- At the end of the time, get the learners to summarise what they read without showing each other their news stories. They both listen for differences – differences in reported facts (one version reports ten people killed, one version states 11 people) or a different angle.

- After speaking about the story, get them to look at each other's version, talk about where the stories came from and what the usual style of this newspaper/website is. Ask them if they have any favourite websites for reading the news.

Follow-up Look at different style features of the two versions – a story from the popular press is likely to use a lot of informal language, idioms and slang and will probably contain quite dramatic language, whereas a story from the quality press will probably be more formal and report more impartially.

Learner autonomy Discuss the benefits of reading the news in English. And encourage them to do it.

Financial statements

Principle Learners need to read financial statements very often. They will understand the figures, but often need help in learning the specialised vocabulary. Get them to explain the meaning of the figures to you – you are not expected to be an expert in finance.

Prepare

Choose an appropriate financial statement from the company's annual report and identify key items of vocabulary. Remember that in every company there will be differences, depending on the type of industry or whether they use US or UK terms.

Look up the definitions of the terms in a financial dictionary or on the internet and make a card-matching activity. Make enough sets of cards for every two learners. For example:

Fixed assets	Long-term assets such as buildings, furniture and machinery
Accounts receivables	Money which is owed to the company by its customers
Financial liability	A debt which must be paid by a certain time according to a contract

Also make a copy of the financial statement you chose for each learner and provide a dictionary of financial terms.

Proceed

- Put the learners into pairs and hand out the 'word' cards first. Get them to discuss which words and phrases they already know the definitions for. After a few minutes, give out the 'definitions' cards for the learners to match.

- Ask them what they know already about their company's latest financial report. Refer to the vocabulary on the cards – Do they know any specifics connected with these things?

- Give them the statement to check if they were right.

- Tell the learners you have come into some money and are thinking of buying shares in their company. You haven't done this before, so you don't know much about this area. Ask them to explain some points: your questions can be as simple as you like, as you are playing the role of non-expert.

- After a couple of examples, get the learners to do the same as a paired roleplay, asking each other questions.

One-to-one You ask all the questions – this can be an excellent opportunity to find out more about their company.

Pre-experience learners Use financial statements from a well-known company. This can also work well with business professionals who come from different companies.

Contract contact

Principle Learners need to read technical documents such as contracts – the language is very specialised but they have to understand the relevant parts in detail. Help with skimming skills so that they can identify the *parts* which they need before working on the *detail*.

Prepare

Get the learners to give you some contracts early in the course so that you have time to prepare the lesson. Tell them that they can black out anything confidential – names of companies or amounts of money – but also reassure them that you will keep the contents confidential.

Look through the contracts and find some legal terms which are used. Think of their plain English equivalents:
- *Herewith* – together with this
- *Party* – someone involved in the contract who is interested in the outcome

Put the words and phrases onto cards – the terms and the definitions. You may need to use a legal dictionary for this, either a printed or online version. Take the dictionary into the lesson. Make sets of cards for every two or three learners, and a copy of the contract for each learner in the group.

Proceed

- Give out the cards and tell the learners to make pairs – the legal terms with the plain English definitions.

- Give out copies of the contract. Set a time limit to read the text and underline the words from the cards (depending on how long the contract is, perhaps work only with part of it). When the time is up, the learners compare in pairs.

- Ask the learners how they deal with reading contracts:
  - Look through the whole contract, look at the headings and decide which parts are most important for them?
  - Skim through the contract for key words – the name of their client?
  - Identify the important parts, then read them in detail using a legal dictionary where necessary?

- They skim the contract to find a section which is very important for them. In pairs, they read it, using a legal dictionary where necessary, and summarise it.

- They then work with a new partner who has read a different part of the contract, give each other a summary of the parts they read and ask each other questions.

Alternative Do this activity with technical manuals – it can be very useful for learners who work in the IT industry.

Higher levels Set up a roleplay around the contract – client and supplier negotiate prices or discuss penalty clauses.

Different dictations

Principle Learners need support when learning how to listen for detail, as well as to read for detail. Do a differentiated listening task in a mixed-level group.

Prepare

Choose a short text as the basis of your dictation and put it onto an OHT or a handout.

Prepare different versions, based on the levels of the group. These examples go from difficult to very easy:

Higher-level learners

Sales figures for 2008

Gapped text

Sales figures … 2008
Yesterday … announced their 2008 sales figures. There was a sharp … of … in the European market. Sales in …, however, … by … . Overall sales … from … to … .

Multiple-choice

Sales figures in 2008
            for
            by

Yesterday The Sun   announced their 2008 sales figures.
         The Mirror
         The Times

There was a sharp rise   of 5% in the European market.
           fall   15%
           increase 50%

Sales in the UK,   however, fell by 3%.
      the US   fall
      the South   dropped

Overall sales went up from 1.5 million to 1.65 million.
            by
            to

Before the lesson, decide which learners are going to work with which version of the text. Put their names on their copies.

Proceed

- Explain the task and read the text aloud at normal speed. Read it a second time.

- The learners check their answers in pairs. They can do this with people who had the same version or a different one.

Follow-up Show the correct version and discuss differences. Use a version similar to the above to review or introduce the language of trends, with a focus on verbs and prepositions.

Preparation makes perfect

Principle Learners need strategies for understanding their business partners, particularly on the telephone. Listening can be difficult because of the lack of visual support, the connection can be poor or the call can be unexpected. Demonstrate the benefits of preparation.

Prepare
Find an authentic recording which is difficult to understand (maximum one minute long) – a short news report or a section from a radio show.

Proceed
- Explain to the learners that they are going to listen to a short recording. Tell them to listen, play the recording, then ask them what it was about. They will find this very difficult, so elicit *why*:
  - They had no idea what they were going to listen to.
  - By the time they had worked it out, it had ended.

- Now give the learners some information about the same recording which will help them prepare to listen to it – *It's a news report about the economy in France.* In pairs, they talk to each other for two minutes and predict what the recording says.

- Play it again and get them to talk about what they heard.

- Explain that prediction helps them to make guesses at gaps in understanding when the sound is poor or vocabulary is lacking.

- In pairs, they think of more ways to make listening easier. Monitor and provide support. One learner can write tips on the board, collected from the group. For example:

- Spend time preparing for a call, if possible – anticipate what the caller might say.
- If it is a telephone conference, read the agenda or find out the topic and brainstorm ideas which might be discussed.
- Ask the caller if you can phone back in a few minutes. Hang up, then spend a couple of minutes preparing.
- Listen out for key words and phrases if you cannot understand every word, and try to guess the rest.
- Use checking and clarifying language: *Do you mean …? So what you are saying is … .*
- Make notes while the other person is speaking.
- Get as much listening practice as possible – by watching DVDs in English and listening to the radio or podcasts.

Review Keep the tips, to refer to in future telephoning and listening lessons. Use the language within the tips (such as checking and clarifying) as your language focus.

Learner autonomy Encourage them to listen regularly to podcasts on the internet.

The CEO's presentation

Principle Learners need to develop skills in listening for gist (the general idea) as well as for details. Use the CEO's presentation at the AGM (annual meeting of shareholders) – in international companies, the presentation will usually be in English and is often available on the company's website or intranet.

Prepare
Find the link to the presentation and watch it. You will either need to download it or have internet access in your lesson. There might also be a script available with the presentation which will make planning the lesson easier. Make sure the presentation is not too long – use an extract if necessary.

Make cards with simple headings of things the CEO talks about and make one set of cards for every two learners.

Profit	Recent acquisitions
Sale of rights to brand X	New opportunities

Proceed
- Put the learners into pairs to brainstorm what they think the CEO will talk about in the speech, from their knowledge of the past year's business.

- Hand out the cards and get the learners to work out exactly what the CEO will say about each subject.

- They watch the presentation to see if they were correct, then talk in pairs about what the CEO really did say about the subjects on the cards, and anything else they can remember – you may want the learners to watch the presentation more than once.

- If available, you can refer to the script from the presentation for the learners to check their answers.

Business professionals Use a presentation from a competing company.

Pre-experience learners Use the CEO's presentation from a well-known international company.

Annual reports

Principle Learners need to be able to talk about current company events, using relevant vocabulary – an annual report is an ideal way of finding this information. Break down the report into manageable chunks and make it more accessible to learners of all levels.

Prepare

Annual reports are usually very large documents. It can be difficult to know where to start if a learner brings one to the lesson. So ask probing questions *before* the lesson, to identify which parts are important. Once you have identified them, prepare five questions. Make enough copies of the chosen section for each learner in the group and a copy of the questions for every two learners.

Proceed

- Put the learners into pairs. Give each pair a copy of the annual report and the questions. They work together and answer the questions. Confirm the answers.

- Set them the task of making up their own five questions.

- Once completed, they exchange their questions with another pair and find the answers.

Higher levels With shorter sections of the report, get the learners to write their own questions on a different section – if you started with the letter from the CEO, they can work on other sections to write their questions, and this way they become familiar with more sections of the annual report as they go through the lesson.

Lower levels Don't be too ambitious. The language of an annual report is often complex, the report lengthy and the learners could feel frustrated and demotivated. Make sure your five questions are graded to the learners' level – *Who is this letter to?* Review question forms or give prompts, to help the learners make their own questions – or leave out this stage altogether if necessary.

Advertising

Principle Salespeople need to use language which attracts people's attention and makes them want to know more about their products or services. Write promotional emails – but cover email writing skills first.

Prepare

Get the learners to give you adverts and publicity material on their company – leaflets, flyers, brochures, posters, even short video films – early in the course so that you have time to prepare the lesson.

Pick out one or two useful advertising phrases. Depending on the product or the company and what format the material is, they could be phrases such as 'outstanding delivery times', 'serving individual needs', 'the very highest quality', 'the latest technology'. Make sure you have enough material for every two learners, or make copies.

Proceed

- Discuss the advertising material with the learners. Have they already read it? Who is the intended reader – members of the public, shareholders, one particular target customer? Is it a good advert? Look at the pictures, the layout and the format during the short discussion.

- Focus on the typical advertising phrases you found. Ask the learners to look through the advert and find some more phrases.

- Tell them they are going to send an email campaign about one of their products. Elicit a suitable way to start the email and write this on the board:
    Dear partner,
    We are sure you are happy working with our model XYZ and we would like to you let you know about some exciting new developments in our range.

- In pairs, they complete the email, using as many phrases as possible from the adverts. Monitor and help out.

- When they have finished, get one pair to exchange with another, to check who used the most advertising phrases.

Alternative If you have access to computers in the classroom, show TV adverts – many companies have their TV adverts on their websites. The learners use these to find examples of advertising language they might be able to use in their own emails.

Follow-up Ask the learners to bring adverts from some of the company's competitors to the lesson. They compare and contrast the adverts with their own and discuss the differences. The group could agree a list of criteria on which to judge the advertisements – layout, overall impression and choice of language – and decide on the 'best'.

Real emails

Principle Business professionals need to write emails quickly but accurately in terms of grammar, vocabulary and style. Authentic emails are often very similar – so they can re-use phrases. Show them some ways of making this easier, as well as creating sources of other useful phrases.

Prepare
Ask the learners to bring some emails which they have written or received in English and which are typical for their jobs. These can include emails written by colleagues which they were copied in on.

Proceed
- Put the learners into pairs to read the emails and underline any phrases they think could be used again in another email. Preferably, put people together who do similar jobs or work in the same department.

- Get them to feed back to the group and to talk about the phrases they have found. As the others listen, they make a note of any phrases which might be useful.

- At the end of the activity, they should have lots of notes of useful phrases. Tell them to type these up for homework and email them to you or bring them next lesson – this way you can check that all the phrases are accurate (sometimes they find phrases in emails from other non-native speakers which contain errors).

- Look at the phrases they send to you, make any necessary corrections and email them back or give them back in the next lesson. Give feedback as appropriate.

One-to-one Sit at the learner's computer and work with their in-box, getting them to choose phrases and to cut and paste them directly into a document which they can then save for future reference.

Follow-up Get the learners to email their documents to each other periodically to see if they can cut and paste anyone else's phrases onto their list. Also get them to ask colleagues who do similar jobs for copies of their emails to check if they can use any of their phrases.

Learner autonomy Tell them to save their list of phrases as a document they can easily access. Next time they have to write an email in English, they should refer to it and cut and paste any phrases which might be useful. Encourage them to keep adding to this document when they come across new phrases.

Model report

Principle Learners need to write reports which look professional and include all the features expected in the genre – an especially important skill for auditors who have to write up their findings. While there are lots of features general to all audit reports, there will also be company guidelines and company-specific requirements to take into consideration. Train the learners to identify such features.

Prepare
Get the learners to provide you with a copy of the company guidelines (if applicable and if in English) and a copy of a final report someone else has written – do this early in the course so that you have time to prepare. If possible, try to find an audit report on the internet (government departments have audit reports available to the public) and make copies along with the company guidelines. Look through the report and do the activity first yourself before the lesson.

Make a copy of the worksheet for every two learners.

Who will read this report?	
Why will they read it? What information is most important for them?	
What are the sections? What order do they come in?	
What words or phrases are typical of the report?	
What grammatical structures are typical of the report?	

Proceed
- Ask the learners about the reports they have to write. What do they find difficult? What company guidelines do they have to follow?

- Give them the worksheet and a copy of your model audit report. Get them to read the report and answer the questions in pairs. Monitor and provide support where necessary.

- Get the learners to work with a new partner and talk about what they found.

- In feedback, discuss how they can use this information when writing their next report.

Follow-up Ask the learners to bring to the next lesson any reports they are currently writing and work on them together, to see if they match the model.

Vocabulary diary

Principle Advanced learners need to be challenged to expand their range of vocabulary – not only relying on tried and tested words but new options of expression. Encourage them to be pro-active in learning new vocabulary and to make this a regular part of their lives.

Prepare

You need internet access – to look at an online monolingual dictionary – or you need to take a monolingual dictionary into the lesson. And you need an authentic article or text to read.

In the previous lesson, ask the learners to bring in a small notebook, small enough to fit into their pocket or handbag.

Proceed

■ Read the article and ask the learners to choose around five words or phrases they would like to learn. Using the dictionaries, they should find as much information about their word or phrase as possible:
  - Example sentences
  - Collocations
  - Pronunciation
  - Grammatical information
  - Frequency

■ Tell them to make a note of all this information in their new notebooks. Explain that these are their *vocabulary diaries*, which they should use to record new and interesting words or phrases they come across:
  - Something they read
  - Something they hear on TV or on the radio
  - Something they hear someone say

Follow-up Use *How is that word used?* (see opposite) to give more options for investigating new vocabulary.

One-to-one Make this procedure a regular part of the lesson, where the learner tells you what new words and phrases are in their diary.

Review Use these notebooks frequently – the learners can compare their notes with the other group members, telling them about the interesting new vocabulary they have found and finding out what the others have recorded.

Learner autonomy Whenever they have time, encourage them to use a monolingual dictionary and make notes of all the information available.

How is that word used?

Principle Advanced learners need to improve their range of vocabulary, but it can sometimes be difficult to identify exactly how to use useful words. Show them how to use a corpus to investigate actual usage.

Prepare

You need internet access and some vocabulary from recent lessons which your learners identified as being useful to learn – from news articles, their work documents or words you provided. Ideally, get the learners to provide the list of these words.

Proceed

■ Ask the learners about words they have come across recently. Where can they find information on how to use them? From the original context? From a monolingual dictionary?

■ Ask if they have ever seen a language corpus. This is a collection of spoken and written language which has been entered into a database, enabling people to search for words or phrases and see how they are currently being used in English. It gives authentic examples, in the form of a 'concordance', as well as providing interesting information on collocations.

■ Call up a corpus on the internet, eg the British National Corpus on http://www.natcorp.ox.ac.uk/index.xml.

■ The learners type in one of the words on their list and see what the concordance shows.

■ Discuss what interesting information can be seen about this word:
  - Does it have any strong collocations?
  - Is it used as part of a phrase?
  - Is it used as a noun, verb, adjective?
  - What kind of document or conversation do the samples come from?
  - Does this say anything about how the word is used?
  - How common is this word or phrase?

Alternative If you do not have internet access in your lesson, print out some of the examples of concordances and take them in.

Homework The learners can look up more words and tell you in the next lesson any interesting information they have found.

Synonym search

Principle Learners need to be able to use a range of words to make their language more interesting and more sophisticated. Increase their awareness of words with similar meanings, related to their jobs.

Prepare

Create a text on a topic related to your learners' jobs. Ensure that it contains a high frequency of words that are *repeated*. For HR officers who work in recruitment, the text could start:

> *In an interview, a candidate is asked about her previous job. She is also asked about her current job and why she has applied for this job.*

Make one copy of the text for every learner in the group.

Proceed

- Give the learners each a copy of the text: What is wrong with it?
- Put them into groups and get them to brainstorm alternative words – *employment*, *position* – that would improve the text.
- The learners rewrite the text using the synonyms.
- They compare their texts, and vote for the best one.

Business professionals Get the learners to use the alternative vocabulary to talk about their jobs – describing their own career history or talking about their company's products or services.

Pre-experience learners Create a text describing a company or a job all the learners are familiar with.

The specialist

Principle Business professionals need to be able to use vocabulary related to their specialised jobs and industries. Use readily available resources to prepare a presentation or explanation about a particular aspect of their work – the added advantage is that you get a better understanding of what your learners do and can identify areas to help with in the future.

Prepare

Choose an aspect of the learners' jobs which you know is important to them but which you don't fully understand – if teaching bankers, you might choose the stock exchange, investment funds or the risks of international trading.

Tell the learners that you would like them to prepare a presentation/explanation on the chosen topic for homework. Tell them that it should be simple enough for a non-expert to understand.

Explain that there might be some vocabulary they do not know, and elicit places they can look to find this – the internet, company literature or specialist dictionaries.

Proceed

- Get the learners to give their presentation to you. Ask lots of questions, especially about vocabulary – *What exactly is a 'derivative'?* In their explanations, the learners will be forced to use a lot of specialist vocabulary.
- They should have informed themselves about a lot of the vocabulary in the preparation stage, but in the lesson allow them to help each other and share the knowledge they possess.
- Make a note of the useful vocabulary which comes up, for revision in future lessons.

Alternative If the learners are reluctant to do homework, get them to do the preparation stage in the lesson, but remember you will need to have the resources at hand – an internet connection or specialist dictionary.

Business professionals In classes where learners do different jobs or come from different industries, get them to prepare presentations/explanations for each other and ask follow-up questions.

Collocations cards

Principle Learners need to be able to use vocabulary accurately in conjunction with other words. Raise their awareness of the importance of word partnerships – rather than focusing on single words – and make their language sound more natural.

Prepare

Find a text on a relevant subject, or get the learners to provide one. Choose some collocating words and put them on cards. Examples of some possible HR collocations:

personal	development
selection	process
compile	a shortlist
invite	to an interview

Make one set of cards for every two or three learners. Prepare 'gist' and 'specific-information' tasks, making a copy of your text and the questions for every learner in the group.

Proceed

■ Give out the text, get the learners to complete the reading tasks and then discuss the content.

■ Give out the collocations cards. The learners make pairs and check their answers by looking at the text, explaining the meaning of the words from the context.

Alternative Give out the cards *before* the learners read the text, telling them to put them into pairs to form collocations. They then check them when they read the text.

Follow-up The learners choose collocations from the lesson and use these to write their own description of the selection process.

Review Give out the cards again in a future lesson. The learners see if they can remember the collocations, then use them as prompts to summarise what the text was about.

This activity can also work well to fill in any absentees on what they missed.

Learner autonomy Only use collocations from the first half of the text when you prepare the cards, then get the learners to identify their own collocations in the rest. Encourage them to do this with material they read in English in their own time.

Collocations prompts

Principle Learners need to build up a whole range of active collocations related to their specialist areas. Show them how to use a collocations dictionary and demonstrate the benefits.

Prepare

Look up a key word that is related to your learners' jobs in a collocations dictionary – if they work for an insurance company, look up the word 'insurance'. Make a note of useful collocations. Divide these words into parts of speech (nouns, verbs, etc). Provide a collocations dictionary for every three or four learners.

Proceed

■ Write the key word on the board/flipchart. Write the *nouns* that collocate around the word in blue and the *verbs* in red. The example 'insurance' might look like this:

[Blue]   *travel, home, car*   *company, policy, claim*

Insurance

[Red]   *claim, take out, have, issue*

■ Elicit why some words are written in blue and others in red. Explain that you are going to focus on some collocations:
  - Verbs that can combine with the key word to make a verb-noun partnership
  - Nouns that can combine with the key word to make a noun-noun partnership

■ Put the learners into small groups and give them a collocations dictionary. Introduce other collocations by getting the learners to look up other words in the dictionary. For this topic, they might want to look up *claim* or *policy*.

■ They record these words in lists of verb-noun and noun-noun collocations.

■ To practise the language, get the learners to prepare simple example sentences connected with their jobs.

Follow-up As a futher practice activity, the learners use the words to prepare a presentation about their job.

Higher levels Add adjectives and adverbs, once the verb-noun and noun-noun collocations are clear.

Pre-experience learners Use general business words such as *meeting*, *communication* or *company* to produce a list of useful collocations.

Key words

Principle Learners need to be able to pronounce words that are absolutely key to their working context – this will make them sound more professional as well as easier to understand. Use the phonemic alphabet, but only as a reminder – the learners do not have to know the symbols off by heart. They can look them up in the dictionary.

Prepare

Identify words your learners need on a regular basis – features or names of their products or names of departments – and write them on index cards. Provide enough learner dictionaries for every two or three learners in the group, or provide access to an online dictionary.

Proceed

■ Model the activity first. Write one of the words on the board/flipchart. Get one of the learners to look up the word in the dictionary and write the word in phonemic symbols on the board. Show them how to find the stressed syllable – the syllable which comes after the apostrophe in the dictionary – and mark this on the board, too.

■ Drill the word by saying it and getting everyone to repeat it.

■ Give out the cards you have prepared. Get the learners to add the phonemic symbols, using the dictionaries.

■ Put them into pairs to practise saying the words, using the phonemic symbols key in the dictionary if necessary. Monitor to check they have the correct pronunciation.

Review Keep the cards, to use in future lessons as revision.

Learner autonomy Encourage them to add phonemic symbols each time they record new vocabulary – both in class and in their own time.

The expert speaker

Principle Learners need to hear how good speakers use intonation, pauses and sentence stress. Give them a model to help them speak effectively.

Prepare

Find a speech by a very good speaker on the internet. Politicians are a good choice – the presentation can be historical or recent – or you can use a speech from the learners' company or industry – the CEO's annual speech to shareholders. Get the script from the internet or transcribe the section you want to use – double-spaced – and make copies. A section of no more than one minute is enough.

Proceed

■ Lead in to the speech with a prediction activity – Who is speaking? What about? What will they say?

■ Play the speech once, while the learners follow the script.

■ Tell them that they are going to listen again and should mark where the speaker pauses:
- They put one line (/) for a short pause.
- They put lines (//) for a longer pause.

■ Play the speech again – they mark the pauses and then compare with a partner.

■ Tell the learners they are going to listen again and mark on the script which words are *emphasised*. Demonstrate with the first sentence – you play it, the learners underline the stressed words, compare in pairs and then all together. Now play the whole section – they mark the stressed words and compare.

■ Tell them to listen again and mark where the speaker's voice *rises* and *falls*. Demonstrate with the first sentence before doing the whole section – the learners mark 'rising' with ↗ and 'falling' with ↘ and then compare.

■ If necessary, play the whole speech once more for checking.

■ Finally, play the speech again and the learners *read along* with the recording, trying to use the pauses, intonation and sentence stress they have marked.

■ Ask the learners in what situations they should improve their intonation, pausing and sentence stress in their jobs – When giving presentations? When summarising at a meeting? When explaining something over the telephone?

Higher levels Give the transcript with no punctuation at all. This makes it much more challenging to decide where the pauses will come.

One-to-one Follow the same procedure, but give control of the recording to the learner so they can pause and replay as many times as they want.

What mood am I in?

Principle Learners need to widen their intonation range, especially if their first language has a narrower range than English. Let them experiment in the safe environment of the classroom and have some fun – before trying it out in a work situation.

Prepare

Make a set of 'mood' cards for every two or three learners in the group:

unsure	angry
enthusiastic	surprised
bored	concerned
suspicious	impatient

Proceed

- Hold up a card without showing anyone what it says. Tell the learners that it says how you are feeling.

- Tell one learner to ask you a question to which the answer will be 'yes' or 'no'.

- You answer in the way of the card – if the card says 'unsure', your voice will waver up and down when you say *yes* or *no*. They should try to guess how you feel.

- Give out the cards. The learners follow the same procedure in pairs, asking each other *yes/no* questions and replying in the mood on the card.

Lower levels Pre-teach or simplify some of the vocabulary on the cards as necessary.

One-to-one You try to guess the learner's mood.

Meaningful silence

Principle Learners need to speak slowly and clearly, for example when giving a presentation, but nerves can cause them to rush. Encourage them to pause, making it easier for the listeners to follow. This works particularly well with a one-to-one learner who is working on a new presentation.

Prepare

Get the script of a short section of a learner's presentation and make a copy for any other learners. Prepare another copy:

- Mark short pauses at the end of a phrase with /.
- Mark longer pauses at the end of a paragraph with //.

Proceed

- Ask the learner to read out part of their presentation from the script – using the first, unmarked copy.

- Record it.

- Give out the second version with the pauses. Record them reading this version:
  - They pause and count to two at the / marks.
  - They pause and count to five at the // marks.

- Play both versions and discuss how much easier the second version is to understand.

- Get the learner to work on another section of the presentation, adding the / and // marks themselves. Point out where there will often be a pause:
  - After stressed words
  - After signposting words and phrases such as *firstly* or *finally*
  - After making a point and when moving on to the next one

Alternative Word process a section of the learner's presentation. Get them to press 'Enter' wherever a pause should come so that the text starts a new line. They can read out the extract, pausing at the end of each line.

Review Get the learner to practise their presentation and record it for homework. In the following lesson, listen to it together and compare it with their very first recording.

Meaningful stress

Principle Learners need to use 'contrastive stress' to add meaning. In the sentence *I work in London* the most important, and therefore stressed, word is usually *London*. However, if the speaker chooses to stress *work* – 'I *work* in London' – this implies that there is some special significance to that word: perhaps they work in London but live elsewhere. Raise awareness of this even with higher-level learners, who may feel that they already 'know' all the language they need.

Prepare

Have ready ten counters for every two learners in the group, nine in the same colour and one in a different colour. (Alternatively, use ten pieces of coloured card.)

Prepare a number of sentences for the activity.

Proceed

- Write up a sentence relevant to the learners' working context:

  The October sales forecast has to be finished before Friday.

- Ask which word is stressed in this sentence. The learners will probably say 'Friday' (the deadline is the most important information).

- Put the counters in a line – nine of the same colour and one different. This represents the sentence, with the different counter at the end being the stressed word – 'Friday'.

- Tell the learners to move the counters so that the *second* one is different – it is the second word that is now stressed. The sentence is now:

  The *October* sales forecast has to be finished before Friday.

- Elicit the difference in meaning (we are talking about the *October* sales forecast, not the *September* sales forecast).

- In pairs, the learners move the counters around so that different words are stressed – they work out how this changes the meaning. Monitor and help out where necessary.

- Work with the other sentences you've prepared.

Alternative Follow the same procedure – but use questions instead of statements.

A map of my day

Principle Learners need to be able to use basic tenses fluently and accurately. Consolidate the present simple with your elementary learners (but also as revision for higher levels) before comparing with other tenses. Draw out the target language from the learners' professional contexts and practise through a personalised activity.

Proceed

- Write 'Things I do at work' in the middle of the board/ flipchart and draw a circle round it. Elicit examples and make a mindmap:

- Ask the learners what tense we use to talk about things we do every day (present simple) and elicit the form (remember to add *-s* to *he/she/it*). They write some notes about their typical day at work. Monitor, and check for any problems.

- In pairs, get them to tell each other about their days, using their notes.

- Ask one learner for information about their partner's typical day. Check they add *-s* to the third person form.

- Get them to change partners and tell their new partner about their first partner's day.

Follow-up Include adverbs of frequency. Draw a cline on the board and write 0% and 100% at the ends. Using 'never' and 'sometimes' as examples, and ask the learners where they go on the cline. Elicit any other adverbs of frequency they know, and ask where they should go:

Elicit some sentences answering the question *How often do you …?* Include phrases such as 'once/twice/three times a day/month/year' and 'every day'.

In pairs, the learners ask each other *How often do you …?* using the verbs on the mindmap. They answer using adverbs or adverbial phrases of frequency.

One-to-one Get the learner to complete the mindmap with their own ideas, either on the board or on a piece of paper.

Enjoy your meal!

Principle Learners need to build relationships with their professional business partners – including making small talk over lunch. Integrate grammar with the skill of socialising, reviewing and practising the present perfect in a work-related context.

Prepare

Prepare a set of cards and make a set for every two or three learners:

eat	drink	drive	be
visit	see	fly	live

Proceed

■ Elicit questions the learners can ask over a business lunch to make small talk with a foreign visitor – *Is this your first visit to London?*

■ Tell them it is practically inevitable to ask *Have you ever …?* questions. Elicit a realistic context, brainstorm examples of appropriate questions and write them up:
  - *Have you ever eaten Japanese food before?*
  - *Have you ever driven on a German motorway?*

■ Elicit the form (*have* + past participle). You may need to review the irregular forms of the verbs you will be using.

■ Explain that the learners are going to practise making small talk questions. Put them into groups of two or three, and give each group a set of cards. Ask one learner to choose a card. Elicit the 'third form' of the verb and get them to use the verb by asking you a *Have you ever …?* question. Answer and expand on their question:
  - *Have you ever been to Paris?*
  - *Yes, I was there last year.*

■ Elicit what tense you used while answering – the past simple, because you gave a time in the finished past. Model as many times as necessary.

■ Get the learners to work in their groups, taking a card then asking and answering *Have you ever …?* questions. Monitor, and check that they are using the tenses correctly. Make notes of language for feedback with the whole group.

Follow-up Practise the present perfect with 'yet'. Give out some blank cards for each learner to write a place of interest for company visitors. Elicit questions – *Have you seen the Town Hall yet?* They ask the questions, and respond with follow-up questions – *What can you do there?*

Higher levels Encourage the learners to come up with their own questions rather than just responding to card prompts.

Review In the next lesson re-use the cards as a warmer.

Trendsetting

Principle Learners need to recognise key words as 'signals' to help them use different tenses correctly. Focus on these in a 'guided discovery' format. This works especially well after examining the language of trends.

Prepare

Write some sentences, preferably focusing on the learners' company (you can find information on their website). The sentences should use each of the tenses you want to focus on alongside key words. There should be a few examples of each:
  - *Our turnover increases every year in the summer.*
  - *Sales are currently increasing in Asia.*
  - *Profits fell last year.*
  - *Our share prices have increased by 12% since May.*

Make enough copies of the worksheet for each learner:

Name of tense	How do you make it?	When do you use it?	Example sentence	Key words and phrases
Present simple				
Present continuous				
Present perfect				
Past simple				

Proceed

■ Give each learner a copy of your sentences and put them into groups of two or three to decide: Which tense is used? Why? What are the key words in each sentence?

■ In our examples, the key words are:
  - In the first sentence – *every year*
  - In the second sentence – *currently*
  - In the third sentence – *last year*
  - In the last sentence – *since*

■ Elicit other possibilities for each of the tenses:
  - Present simple – *sometimes, always, usually*
  - Present continuous – *at the moment*, *right now*
  - Past simple – *yesterday, in 1991*
  - Present perfect – *since* or *for*

■ Put the learners into pairs and get them to fill in the information on their worksheet. Monitor and help out.

Learner autonomy Tell them to keep this in an accessible place to refer to – for when they are writing emails.

The covering letter

Principle Learners need to be able to use present perfect and past simple correctly so that it is clear whether they are talking about something which is finished or still continuing – a difficult area for many due to first language interference. Demonstrate in the business context of a letter from someone applying for a job.

Prepare

This activity will take some time to create but it is worth it, especially if you have several classes at the same company. Write a covering letter for a job at the company (see below for an example to adapt – an application to a German chemical company). Make copies for every learner.

Proceed

■ Elicit what the duties of an International Marketing Manager could be – What experience and qualifications should such a person have at the learners' company?

■ Say that you have a covering letter from an applicant who applied for the job at their company. You may need to pre-teach vocabulary from the letter.

■ Hand out the letter and tell the learners to read it and decide if the person would be suitable for their company.

■ In small groups, they discuss the advantages and the disadvantages of the candidate:
  • The applicant is working for a competitor.
  • He will have to move a large family overseas.
  • He doesn't speak any German.

■ After the discussion, explain that they are going to focus on some of the grammar in the text.

■ Write the following years on the board:
  1999   2001   2004   2006

■ Get the learners to re-read the text and find out what the candidate did in each of the years.

■ Write the answers on the board to create a timeline:
  1999 – Finished PhD, started working for Competitor 2
  2001 – Got married
  2004 – Stopped working for Competitor 2, moved to NY, started MBA program
  2006 – Ended MBA program, started to work for Competitor 1

■ Elicit the tense used. The learners read the text again to check if the candidate always uses the past simple when talking about his career history, or if he also uses other tenses. If necessary, draw their attention to the sentence *I have worked for Competitor 1 since 2006.*
  What tense is it? (present perfect)
  Why? (The applicant still works for Competitor 1.)

■ Get them to form other sentences in the present perfect, using the dates on the timeline:
  He has been married since 2001.
  He has had an MBA since 2006.

■ Give the learners a few minutes to think about their own career histories and write down important dates on a piece of paper. In pairs, they tell each other what the dates mean, using both the past simple and present perfect. Monitor, and check they are using the tenses correctly.

Lower levels In the final practice stage, the learners write whole sentences including the dates *before* telling each other.

Higher levels The learners write their own covering letter to a company similar to the one they work in now in a country of their choice. They could do this for homework.

Pre-experience learners The learners write a version of the letter based on a famous company they all know.

Review In the next lesson, the learners exchange and read each other's letters, checking the tenses.

Name of the company
Address of the company

Dear Sirs:

I am writing in response to your advertisement for an International Marketing Manager in last week's *Sunday Times*. I am 38 years old and from Argentina. I finished a PhD in Chemistry in 1999 and an MBA from New York University in 2006. I speak fluent English and Spanish, and I have a good knowledge of Portuguese.

I have worked for **[Competitor 1]** in Argentina since 2006, where I am in charge of marketing decorative paints in South America. I have played a key role in helping the company increase its turnover in a very competitive sector. Before I started my two-year MBA program (2004 –2006), I worked for **[Competitor 2]** in Brazil, developing paint for the automobile industry.

Since the start of my career, I have enjoyed working in the chemical industry and especially enjoy the paints sector. I am keen to find a position which combines my experience of marketing and chemistry, and I would particularly like to work with an international company. I got married in 2001 and we now have four children, but we would be happy to live in Germany. My wife is a physiotherapist so she can move easily. We are excited about learning German and living in a new country.

I am hard-working, independent and enjoy a challenge. I can provide full references if necessary. Please find enclosed my resumé.

I look forward to hearing from you soon.

Yours truly,

Bottled!

Principle Learners in technical jobs often need to describe processes. Use a Test-Teach-Test approach to practise the passive.

Prepare

Find a picture of a bottling machine. Make enough copies for every two learners in the group and prepare a simple description of how the machine works. This should include the passive voice and sequencing phrases:

First, the bottles are put on the conveyor belt. Then they are moved along until they are under the juice. Next, the juice is piped into the bottles. After that, they are moved further along and a cap is screwed onto the bottle. Finally, they are packed into boxes of 12.

- **The first Test stage** You can think of different examples for this stage, but it should be a process which is *different* from ones the learners really need to describe.
- **The Teach stage** Be prepared to teach the passive and sequencing phrases as necessary.
- **The second Test stage** Now that you have raised awareness of and taught the passive and sequencing phrases, the learners will do a *real-life* process from their jobs. For this stage, use pictures from their work situation. (Find these on the internet or in company publications.)

Proceed

■ Carry out the three stages as outlined opposite.

Alternative Learners who work in administration may not have enough background information to be able to talk about technical processes. Adapt this activity by using processes that are relevant to their jobs – learners in Human Resources may mention recruiting new staff or sending delegates to a foreign country.

Business professionals Get them to take you into their place of work – the factory – and explain the various production processes.

TEST

- Put the learners into pairs and tell them that you are going to describe a factory where they make a drink called 'SuperJuice'. When the drink is ready, it goes to the bottling machine.
- Give out the pictures of the bottling machine to each pair and elicit/teach the vocabulary the learners will need to describe certain parts – *conveyor belt, to pipe in, to screw on a cap.*
- With their partner, the learners write a short description of how the machine works. Set a time limit of five minutes.
- At the end of the time limit, explain that you are going to dictate *your* description of how the machine works, which they should write down.
- Dictate it, one sentence at a time.
- Get the learners to compare *your* description with *their* version and decide what is different. (They will probably find for themselves more examples of the passive and more sequencing words, but try to guide them towards this.)

TEACH

- Write on the board 'The bottles are put on the conveyor belt'.
- Elicit the *form* of the passive (subject + *to be* + 3rd form) and when it is *used* (when we want to make the object of an active sentence more important by bringing it to the front of the sentence – here, *the bottles*).
- Elicit examples of sequencing words – *first, then, finally* – and write them on the board. Use the examples from your description, but also encourage the learners to think of more – *afterwards, following that, at 9:00.*
- Put the learners into pairs and get them to write a description of a process at work using the passive and sequencing words. Monitor and check.
- Get them to change partners and tell someone else about the process, or to put their descriptions up on the walls and then walk round and read each other's.

TEST

- Put the learners into groups of two or three and give out the pictures of a process from their jobs.
- Get them to write a short description for each process they see in the pictures, making sure they use the passive and sequencing words.
- Monitor whether or not they are using the passive correctly, and give feedback at the end of the activity.
- Get them to exchange their writing with another group, read it to see how similar it is to theirs and check for passives and sequencing words.

The Business English Teacher will have helped you to teach a range of business English learners. By now, you should feel confident dealing with learners at different levels of English and seniority in a company, with learners in different sectors doing different jobs and with groups of various sizes as well as one-to-ones. You should be able to provide them with practical help in improving the English needed in their working lives. You may be starting to wonder how you can continue to develop your own career.

Professional business English teachers are *progress-driven*. Everything you do in the classroom should enable the learners to progress so that they can do their jobs better. This also means that you also need to progress constantly as a teacher. The exciting thing about being a business English teacher is that there is a lot to learn – not only about teaching English but also about business.

The teaching of business English

It is important not to lose sight of the fact that your learners are in your classes to learn English – business English, yes, but English, when all is said and done. Other experts will be teaching them business, or possibly – and most probably – they are already experienced and expert business people themselves.

To progress as a business English teacher, to better teach your business learners, you need to constantly look back at your teaching – to *evaluate* your current classroom practice and reflect on where you can improve – and look forward, with a view to implementing new ideas, new skills and new strategies in the classroom to *improve* on your classroom practice.

The business of teaching English

Teaching business learners is an exciting proposition, as the authors of this book hope you have either realised or even experienced. You may be tempted to make it your speciality, your chosen profession. You may want to take on extra responsibilities. You may decide to make it your own 'business' – as a freelance teacher.

Whatever, you need to continue your learning curve and focus on specific aims and activities that are both rewarding professionally and satisfying personally. Not only *can* you learn more in your field – you *need* to. It is an exciting business – but it is also a serious business.

1 The teaching of business English		**2** The business of teaching English	
Looking back	**Looking forward**	From reading to writing	From training to teacher training
Observation	Action planning	From conferences to courses	From business classroom to business world
Feedback	Course planning	From examinations to examining	

The teaching of business English

Looking back

When your teaching is based on your learners' needs, there is always a new need to meet, a vocabulary topic that you haven't taught before, a work document that you haven't exploited before – one of the exciting things about being a business English professional is that there are always new things to learn.

That said, teaching business English is not a question of being predominantly *re-active*. You will only develop through *pro-active*, systematic analysis of what you do (well or otherwise) now – and what you can do better in the future.

Let us begin by reflecting on a course that you recently taught. This can be any course, whether a group or a one-to-one. For each of the following questions, give yourself a mark between 1 and 5 (1 is the lowest, 5 the highest).

• Did you spend time before the first lesson gathering information about the company and the individual learners?	
• Did you prepare a first lesson that enabled you to get to know your learners and their needs?	
• Did you set clear course objectives and communicate them to the learners?	
• Did you refer to the course objectives when making decisions about individual lesson aims?	
• Did you plan the individual lessons to make them as relevant to the learners' jobs as possible?	
• Did you teach vocabulary relevant to your learners' jobs and exploit the work documents that the learners brought?	
• Did you take on a monitoring role, in order to give the learners as much speaking practice as possible?	
• Did you promote learner autonomy and give the learners tools for practising English outside the classroom?	
• Did you plan regular review sessions?	
• Did you assess the learners' progress throughout the course and give them feedback at the end on where they had made progress and how they can still improve?	

Go through the checklist again. Is there a particular area where it would be useful to concentrate your attention in order to make progress?

- Do you find it difficult to set course objectives with your learners?
- Do you feel unsure how to exploit work documents or how to teach specialist vocabulary?
- Do you tend to talk a lot in the lessons, not giving the learners enough opportunity to speak?
- Do you find it awkward to give the learners feedback on their progress at the end of the course?

There are no set answers to these questions. If you gave yourself a low mark for any one of them, you may find it useful to refer back to the relevant section of this book and/or to talk to more experienced colleagues. Eventually, you will find your own answers and move forward as a teacher by reflecting, experimenting and being open to feedback both from your peers and managers as well as from the business people that you train.

Business people in the business world are expected to constantly improve their skills and work on their weaknesses. It is no different for the business English teacher. However, you may not get the opportunity to have an appraisal with your manager where you set targets for the next year – as your learners will – so you need to take responsibility for your own development. Use all your lessons to progress as a teacher – through *observation* and *feedback*.

Observation

Self-observation – evaluating yourself – is an extremely valuable way of developing, and can be done by making field notes during the lesson on how a stage or activity is going, by filling in a questionnaire or checklist, or by filming yourself teaching. The results can be enlightening.

Field notes can literally be scribbled notes on the side of your lesson plan or on a sheet of paper and might comment on how the learners are engaging with a task or using the target language in an activity. Your comments can help you to identify your strengths and the areas you need to work on:

- *Good instructions. Learners all immediately engaged.*
- *I just corrected Simon without letting him self-correct.*
- *I didn't wait for the group to peer-correct.*

The best questionnaire will involve very short questions that give a graded answer (5 for very good, 1 for very bad) or a checklist. This helps focus your observation during the lesson without distracting you from your actual teaching. The questions will depend on what exactly you are focusing on. For example, if you have identified that you need to pay more attention to how and how often you correct errors, take something like this into the classroom:

How often did I ...	Never	Sometimes	Often
elicit self-correction?			
elicit peer-correction?			
correct on the spot?			
make a note for correction later?			
ignore an error because it was not important?			

You may notice that certain correction *techniques* dominate. Another questionnaire could focus on the learners' contributions. Using a list of names and putting a mark next to them every time they speak might show that it is certain *people* who dominate discussions – and help you to focus on quieter learners.

If you record or film your lesson (or part of it), get your employer's *and* the company's permission – and then ask the learners if they agree, carefully explaining your reasons for doing it. Watching or listening to yourself provides extremely valuable information. How clear are your instructions? How much speaking do *you* do and how much do the *learners* do? Do the group members interact with each other? Is there some of your body language you were previously unaware of?

Peer-observation – another pair of eyes – can offer suggestions and solutions which you may not have thought of. Also, watching someone else's lesson can give *you* fresh ideas. Of course, you will need to check with the learners that they do not mind an extra person being there. When you explain the reasons – the observation is to give you feedback on your teaching and to check the quality of the course – business people will usually be impressed, as it shows your organisation is professional and you are serious about your teaching.

Give your colleague some background information and a task to focus the discussion after the lesson – either concentrate on a specific area of your teaching (possibly from the ideas generated by your self-observation) or a more general one. Remember to do the same task yourself as a *self*-assessment after the lesson – to compare your own ideas with your colleague's. Specific tasks could be:

- **Aims** Was your observer able to identify the lesson and stage aims from their observation (perhaps you don't give them a lesson plan)? If what you are doing is not obvious to an experienced colleague, then it certainly won't be obvious to the learners.
- **Balance of activities and pace** What activity was happening (pair, individual, whole-group, writing, card-matching, mingling)? How long did each stage last? This could highlight your preference for a certain kind of activity at the expense of another.
- **Work transfer** What can the learners take away from the lesson into the workplace? How does the observer know? (If it isn't obvious to them, it won't be to the learners either.)

Feedback should always be developmental and supportive, and the observer should certainly talk about strengths as well as identify areas for development.

Formal observation If you are working for a school, they will often carry out regular observations, involving your DoS, ADoS or centre manager sitting in on the lesson, followed by a feedback discussion. This normally begins by you talking about your impression – what you were pleased with, and what you might change if you had the chance to do the lesson again. The verbal feedback will often be followed by a written summary which both you and your observer agree on. Practical and realistic suggestions should be included and discussed.

The most important thing is to teach a lesson which is typical for you. Don't spend hours preparing materials if you would not normally do that, and don't teach in a completely different style just because someone is watching. You need to get feedback on what you do in a typical lesson. While you will probably write out a more formal lesson plan for an observed lesson, remember that you do not have to stick firmly to your plan if something arises in the lesson – you should always prioritise your learners' needs. If a learner arrives with a story about a meeting she went to that week in English, you should certainly acknowledge this even if it means starting your planned lesson a little later.

Feedback

Learner feedback This is another way of getting external feedback on your teaching. Learner feedback can be *informal* – asking questions at the end of the lesson about how they thought it went.

You can also collect more *formal* feedback in writing, which can encourage the learners to think more deeply about their opinion or to be more honest – especially if it is anonymous. This feedback can be very constructive, but needs to be set up correctly so that the comments you get are useful.

One way of collecting formal feedback is by using tick boxes:

The teaching of business English

	Agree	Not sure	Disagree
My teacher gave me enough chances to speak.			
I understood what I had to do in every activity.			
My teacher did a lot of different activities.			
I learned something which I can use in my job.			

The advantage of this type of feedback is that it is simple and quick for the learners to fill in, as well as for you to look through. You can easily spot trends – if a lot of learners think the lesson was not relevant to their jobs, you need to work more on integrating work-related tasks or help them see how to transfer the language to their daily work.

The main disadvantage of tick boxes is that there is no room for comment. Asking open questions (*In what way was today's lesson useful in your daily work? Why? Did you feel confident expressing your opinion in the lesson? Why not?*) can give you more valuable feedback, as the learners can give details of why they have a certain opinion. It takes longer to fill in – the learners may not see this as being a good use of their lesson time – so be sure to explain the purpose, assuring them that you will use the information to make adjustments to the course.

Corporate feedback Many language schools and companies have their own feedback system which they use to monitor the quality of training. It normally involves having learners fill out feedback forms at the end of the course, the aim of the company being to determine if they are getting a good return on their investment – that their employees are becoming better able to use English in the workplace. This feedback is also extremely useful to you, as you can determine how satisfied the learners were with your course and spot areas for improvement.

However, as it is carried out at the end of the course, it is often too late to make changes. So do not be afraid of doing your own feedback *throughout* the course, on top of an official feedback scheme. (You may wish to inform the company of your intentions.) Business people will be impressed to be asked for feedback from time to time, as it shows that lessons are professional and that you, or the school you represent, care about 'quality control'.

Finally, remember to *use* the information you get, otherwise your learners will certainly *not* be impressed. If they tell you their lessons lack variety, then you should work hard to include a wider range of activities in future. Feedback is a great opportunity to really develop your teaching – and to prove (to yourself and to them) that you are meeting your learners' needs.

Blended learning Amongst your feedback, 'blended learning' may be suggested – perhaps by the company HR manager, perhaps by the learners themselves (or it may be simply an idea of your own). Blended learning is the combination of face-to-face lessons with elements of online work.

Blended learning may match the expectations of business learners who are usually conversant with the latest technology and may expect to see it used in their English courses. It can also offer cost savings to companies – if the learners are able to effectively supplement their language practice using an online platform.

Teaching successful blended courses demands a specialised pedagogy. This is beyond the remit if this book. The authors, therefore, are happy to refer you to *Teaching Online* by Nicky Hockly and Lindsay Clandfield, also published in this series.

The teaching of business English

Looking forward

Now that you have thought about your teaching *so far*, and become more familiar with your strengths and weaknesses, you can look forward to how you can develop what you do in the classroom *from now on*.

Action planning

Having identified areas in your teaching you want to work on, it is important to prioritise and set realistic and specific short-term goals which are achievable within a realistic and measurable time limit. For error-correction, a target could be: 'I have found it difficult to teach financial English. Over the next four weeks I will make an effort to read the financial news, look at financial vocabulary in coursebooks and ask a more experienced teacher to support me.'

You also need to decide how you can monitor your progress. At the end of the period of time, you can do the following:
- Ask to be observed again, either officially or by a peer.
- Do another self-observation or ask your learners for feedback.

Once you have made satisfactory progress in this area, return to the *Looking back* section – and find your next area for development.

Course planning

Another way you can develop is by getting experience in course planning. This means thinking about the learners' overall course aims and planning a series of lessons which will help achieve them, rather than simply thinking about what to do week by week. Course plans give structure – they help *you* when you plan lessons and help your *learners* to see that they are working towards their goals.

Before writing a course plan, you need to decide on the teaching points. We recommend planning for the first eight to ten lessons – and keeping the following in mind:
- The level of the learners in the group.
- The needs of the learners – these will be identified by them (often work-related) and identified by you, often language-related needs.
- Topics the learners are interested in – if several of the learners work in the marketing department, topics that are related to marketing are an obvious choice.
- Business skills – for a block of ten lessons, we suggest limiting it to two business skills at most. Can you link the business skill to the topics? Or to the language work? What aspect of the skill will you work on?
- Language skills that the learners need to develop – try to have a balance of reading, writing, speaking and listening activities. However, if they specifically request working on one skill, include more work on that.
- Language – take into account vocabulary items that are specific to the learners' jobs as well as general vocabulary. How are you going to integrate grammar into the lessons? Will you simply deal with problem areas when they come up?
- Balance – even if the learners say that presentations are their main priority, don't have all your lessons focusing on presentations.
- Learner autonomy – integrate strategies for increasing the learners' contact with English, and show them how to become more independent learners.
- Reviewing and recycling – learners need to revisit language regularly so that they can learn it. We recommend making the last lesson of a block a review lesson, and to include review activities each lesson throughout the course.

The teaching of business English

Once you have decided on the content, you can begin to sequence it. Which topics make the most sense to put at the beginning of the course? Which ones at the end?

- You might find it makes sense to have a lesson that promotes learner autonomy at the beginning of a block of lessons, so that the learners practise the strategy throughout the course.
- You might want to focus on an aspect of grammar after a lesson on presentations, so that you can look at specific grammar errors that they made while presenting.

If you go back to our original email scenario in Part A, a course plan for the group at *JCD International* could be as follows:

Company: JDC International

Objectives:

- To be able to talk about jobs and responsibilities
- To extend the range of finance and HR vocabulary
- To be able to give a presentation about company products
- To be able to participate in negotiations about work-related topics

---

Lesson one:	Needs analysis / Setting objectives
Lesson two:	Describing your company / Talking about your job Strategies to learn vocabulary
Lesson three:	Vocabulary and discussion – Focus: HR
Lesson four:	Vocabulary and discussion – Focus: Finance
Lesson five:	Presentations: Language and practice
Lesson six:	Presentations: Work-related practice
Lesson seven:	Grammar: Problem areas
Lesson eight:	Negotiations: Language and practice
Lesson nine:	Negotiations: Language and practice
Lesson ten:	Review / Plan new course block

You can now type up your plan so that it looks as professional as possible. Bring it into the lesson and share it with your learners. Does your plan meet their expectations? You will find that you will need to be flexible, as perhaps one learner who really wants to do presentations won't be able to attend the presentation lesson – or another learner wants to do negotiations early, to help her with her job. The important thing is to refer to your plan regularly and use it as a discussion tool, so that you are sure that you are meeting your learners' needs and expectations.

Finally, before moving on to the next section, perhaps take the time to do one of the following reflection tasks:

- Think about a group that you are teaching right now. Write up a complete plan for this group.
- Think about a group that requests the following: banking vocabulary, speaking practice and the language of presentations. Plan the first ten lessons of the course.

Where do you feel you need to progress, in order to *teach* either of the plans?

The business of teaching English

We have looked at some length at development in the context of the classroom and the course. Let us now look (albeit briefly) at the enormous and varied career potential afforded by business English teaching – potential for which you will need preparation and planning, and no little dedication and decision-making.

From reading to writing

Reading can be a great asset to progressing as a business English teacher – and it can be more exciting than it sounds. Regularly reading the business section of newspapers will keep you abreast of major business trends and topics that could be of interest to your learners. For more in-depth insight you could subscribe to a business newspaper or magazine such as *The Economist* or *Financial Times*.

You can find books on business that are highly relevant to *teaching* business English – books on presentation skills, negotiation, business writing. They give you helpful hints that you can bring into your lessons. Management self-help books or biographies of successful business people can also be a rich source of business information.

Professional journals and websites for English teachers are a good way of collecting ideas and understanding current trends in the field of TEFL. There are also many online discussion groups available. They also enable you to find out about what is being published and about training events and jobs. Seek out and test the latest published materials for business English. When doing so, reflect on them critically:

- What are the principles and approaches of the author(s)?
- What is useful for you and your learners? What isn't? Why?

Methodology books can be expensive to buy and time-consuming to read. However, it is possible to be selective, to dip into them and read parts relevant to you. They can be an invaluable resource when working to improve your understanding of language or to help you in aspects of self-reflection and development.

If you enjoy writing your own classroom materials, why not dedicate more time to creating them – and then sharing them? Contact professional journals, magazines and websites to see if you can get published. You won't make a fortune (!) but it could lead to new and interesting opportunities. It is generally considered easier to publish online. If your ideas are popular, you might be invited to trial new materials for publishers.

From conferences to courses

IATEFL (International Association of Teachers of English as a Foreign Language) has a Special Interest Group focused on business English teachers: BESIG. There is a BESIG conference once a year somewhere in Europe which includes a variety of training sessions, workshops, discussions and book promotions.

You can take courses on topics that are relevant to teaching *business English* – but you can also take courses (whether online or face-to-face) on topics relevant to teaching *business*.

Business English Many organisations offer courses for Business English teachers on topics such as legal English, technical English and blended learning. Going to conferences and checking professional journals and websites will enable you to get more information about such courses – both face-to-face and, more and more, online.

Business These can be courses on skills which are directly applicable to Business English teaching such as presentations or PowerPoint. Local business colleges often offer such courses. You can take business courses – in time-management, organisation, etc – which would help you to specialise in one particular area.

The business of teaching English

From examinations to examining

Many business English professionals start their careers with an initial teacher training course to gain a basic EFL qualification – for example the Cambridge CELTA and Trinity Cert TESOL. Such qualifications demonstrate to the school that you have a basic understanding of teaching and basic language awareness. They also demonstrate to clients, who are often well-qualified themselves, that you are competent. However, these qualifications are for general EFL teaching.

For specialised business English qualifications, there are several courses available now, intended as a follow-up to the initial certificate course, for example the Trinity Cert IBET and the International House BET. A quick internet search will show a range of options, both for distance and face-to-face learning.

After teaching for a few years, teachers may want to do a diploma-level qualification, for example the Cambridge DELTA or Trinity DipTESOL. Although these in-depth qualifications are also not specifically aimed at business teachers, they cover syllabus design and catering for individual learners' needs, and there are options for taking modules which do focus on business English.

The main business English exam for *learners* is the Cambridge Business English Certificate (BEC). Examiners for the written and spoken papers are often required. Apart from supplementing your income, becoming an examiner is an invaluable way of getting a real understanding of the demands of the exam, if you teach exam courses. With greater insight, you should be able to prepare more relevant and helpful activities for your learners and, by doing so, increase their chances of success.

From training to teacher training

For many teachers of business English, attending training sessions is difficult – you may be a freelancer or simply because you are working in a remote area. However, it is worth trying hard to get training. It gives you the opportunity to gain new ideas and keep up-to-date with new developments. It also gives you the chance to see experienced trainers in action. Training also offers the opportunity to network and to be exposed to practice, ideas, methodologies and approaches outside the institution(s) you work for. Training is certainly an important influence in your development.

Large and well-organised schools often offer *internal* training. To get *external* training, keep an eye out for book promotions in your local area: publishers sometimes combine training sessions with book presentations. In larger cities, there may be an English teachers' association which offers training and discussion forums where you can share ideas.

Leading a training session, perhaps at a school you are working for, can be a good way to get started on the road to becoming a teacher trainer. You can also offer to lead sessions at local English teachers' associations or at conferences such as the IATEFL BESIG.

From business classroom to business world

You have thought about where you are at the moment and how you can develop your classroom practice, and have begun to think about how you can continue to develop professionally and personally – beyond the classroom.

For some people, it is important not just to broaden their skills and experience but to make a career move in the field of business English teaching. What career opportunities are there? Different countries, different educational systems and different individual personalities and possibilities mean that we cannot enter into detail beyond, perhaps, a basic two-fold simplification:

The business of teaching English

Inside an organisation

Within a language school or university, there are a lot of opportunities to progress. Many teachers in language schools climb the career ladder in their own or another institution. These include positions such as:

- Full-time contracts with language schools
- Positions in pedagogical management – Senior Teacher, Assistant Director of Studies (ADoS) or Director of Studies (DoS)
- Management – being the centre manager for a language school

To get a good overview of what is possible, look at a variety of job descriptions and adverts. Once you have identified the professional direction you want to take, find support. Start with where you work:

- Is there a mentoring system or other form of support? An appraisal system?
- What about the DoS/Manager? Can you talk to them and get their advice?
- What about online support? Discussion groups and blogs?

Outside an organisation

You may find it more exciting to work on your own and to build up your own business. This means seeking potential clients, getting the clients and keeping them happy. This will involve:

- Finding a 'niche' and distinguishing yourself from the rest
- Marketing yourself and your services
- Creating a favourable professional 'business-friendly' appearance
- Creating a professional website to offer your services
- Building a portfolio of clients
- Building a bank of materials that only you have at your disposal

In a freelance context, there are probably even more stakeholders to keep satisfied – not only your learners, but company bosses or HR personnel, all with their specific demands: expectations and results, learner progress and learner satisfaction, feedback forms, mid-course appraisals, final evaluations and efficient financial administration. And as your business grows, you may have to consider hiring staff and teachers!

But no matter which direction you choose to go in – to climb up the ladder of an organisation or to strike out on your own and build up your own business, you have to be willing to accept challenges – to take advantage of opportunities that come your way.

To finish *The Business English Teacher*, let us imagine that you receive this email:

○ ○ ○

Hi,

The HR manager at JCD has renewed the contract with a new series of lessons, and they insist that you take the course. I am counting on you!

And by the way, we are employing some new teachers to cover the range of in-company courses we are going to offer. We need an ADoS with a good track record in business English.

Could you come and see me? Let's talk about it.

Regards,

From the editors

The Business English Teacher is a book not only for teachers who are thinking of making a move into the field of business English teaching. It is also for those current practitioners who would like to increase their skills and develop their potential.

All three authors have extensive experience in different areas of business English teaching and have put together a comprehensive and practical guide to being a better and more confident and successful teacher – in a variety of teaching contexts.

- What is a business English teacher? A reassuring yet challenging combination of general English teacher and teacher of specific skills – whose guiding principle is always the needs of the learners.
- What is the underlying pedagogy? The authors look into *who* you teach, *what* you teach, *where* you teach and, in consequence and above all, *how* you can teach confidently and successfully.

- What do you want to know? A series of answers to 'frequently asked questions' that beset teachers who are about to become business English teachers.
- What can you do? A wealth of practical activities that cover the business skills your learners need to perform, and the language skills they need to perform them.

- How can you develop? A look at the need for reflecting on your present classroom performance, through observation and feedback, and for dedicated future planning.
- Where can you develop? A look at the routes you can take in furthering your career, in both the business English teaching world – and the business world.

In short, *The Business English Teacher* is a compendium of good practice and enthusiastic encouragement for teachers who might want to make business English teaching 'their business' – a business as challenging as it is rewarding, both professionally and personally.

Mike Burghall
Lindsay Clandfield

From the publisher

DELTA TEACHER DEVELOPMENT SERIES

A pioneering new series of books for English Language Teachers
with professional development in mind.

Teaching Online
by Nicky Hockly with Lindsay Clandfield
ISBN 978-1-905085-35-4

The Business English Teacher
by Debbie Barton, Jennifer Burkart
and Caireen Sever
ISBN 978-1-905085-34-7

Culture in our Classrooms
by Gill Johnson and Mario Rinvolucri
ISBN 978-1-905085-21-7

Being Creative
by Chaz Pugliese
ISBN 978-1-905085-33-0

The Developing Teacher
by Duncan Foord
ISBN 978-1-905085-22-4

Teaching Unplugged
by Luke Meddings and Scott Thornbury
ISBN 978-1-905085-19-4

For details of future titles in the series,
please contact the publisher or visit the DTDS website at
www.deltapublishing.co.uk/titles/methodology/delta-teacher-development-series

---

Also from DELTA PUBLISHING

professional perspectives
A series of practical methodology books designed to provide teachers of English
with fresh insights, innovative ideas and original classroom materials.

Creating Conversation in Class
by Chris Sion
ISBN 978-0-953309-88-7

Talking Business in Class
by Chris Sion
ISBN 978-1-900783-64-4

Challenging Children
by Henk van Oort
ISBN 978-1-900783-93-4

The MINIMAX Teacher
by Jon Taylor
ISBN 978-0953309-89-4

Dealing with Difficulties
by Luke Prodromou and Lindsay Clandfield
ISBN 978-1-905085-00-2

The Resourceful English Teacher
by Jonathan Chandler and Mark Stone
ISBN 978-0-953309-81-8

Humanising your Coursebook
by Mario Rinvolucri
ISBN 978-0-954198-60-2

Unlocking Self-expression through NLP
by Judith Baker and Mario Rinvolucri
ISBN 978-1-900783-88-0

Spontaneous Speaking
by David Heathfield
ISBN 978-1-900783-92-7

Using the Mother Tongue
by Sheelagh Deller and Mario Rinvolucri
ISBN 978-0-954198-61-9

Please contact the publisher for further details:
Tel +44 (0)1306 731770   *E-mail* info@deltapublishing.co.uk
Web www.deltapublishing.co.uk